DEATH
IN THE
SCHOOL COMMUNITY:

A HANDBOOK FOR COUNSELORS, TEACHERS, AND ADMINISTRATORS

Martha D. Oates, EdD

5999 Stevenson Avenue
Alexandria, VA 22304-3300

American Counseling Association
5999 Stevenson Avenue
Alexandria, VA 22304

Cover Design by Sarah Jane Valdez
Cover Art by Michael Comlish

              Library of Congress Cataloging-in-Publication Data

Oates, Martha D.
  Death in the school community : a handbook for counselors,
teachers, and administrators / Martha D. Oates.
      p.   cm.
  Includes bibliographical references and index.
  ISBN 1-55620-099-4
  1. Children and death. 2. Bereavement in children. 3. Children—
Counseling of. 4. Counseling in education. I. Title.
BF723.D3037 1992
371.4′6—dc20   92-21966
                                                            CIP

Printed in the United States of America

This book is dedicated to
my mother and father

Delia Pearce Holloway

and

Dale Allen Holloway
(1908–1975)

Contents

CHAPTER 6

CONCLUSION

APPENDIX A

APPENDIX B

Foreword

Death in the School Community: A Handbook for Counselors, Teachers, and Administrators is written for professionals who are in the position to guide reactions to a death occurring within a school community. It makes two important assumptions.

First, organized groups of individuals, such as schools, businesses, churches, and volunteer/fraternal organizations, develop extrautilitarian norms and values that go beyond the strict boundaries of group goals. These unwritten norms typically encompass awareness and concern for group members as human beings. Many groups genuinely care about their members' well-being. Other groups, however, never develop a personal level of group concern, and members suffer and are diminished by this organizational indifference. In any case, significant losses by death or separation within the group affect the entire group, not just members individually or uniquely but as group members who share a common identification. An organized group response that represents a communal reaction to such losses and an effort to support group members is possible as well as helpful. This is the meaning behind the concept of *group survivorship* and the essential theme of this book.

Group survivorship is an expansion of the needs individuals and family groups experience in grief. Members of an organized group and its subunits especially touched by the death of a member have the *right* to be acknowledged and recognized as survivors, as having suffered a loss; to be informed of facts concerning the death and subsequent actions taken; and to be allowed to participate in traditional or in creative leave-taking ceremonies. Furthermore, a survivor group has an *obligation* to acknowledge publicly the group's survivorship status; to make a tangible response to immediate family survivors on behalf of the group; and to make such a response within the group to benefit group members.

Second, *Death in the School Community* illustrates the imperative need to plan ahead for a group response to significant loss. Groups such as branches of the military, fraternal organizations, and many

religious organizations have firmly established traditions for responding to a member's death. Our schools tend to be less tradition-bound
and have relatively fewer experiences upon which to draw for guidance
when a member death occurs. But, if we as educators believe that
knowledge empowers and ignorance weakens, we cannot allow ourselves to be "taken by surprise" when a sudden death commands our
attention to act.

Why wouldn't groups naturally want to plan for a death emergency? Some group leaders do not appreciate or recognize the group's
responsibility for member well-being. These leaders simply don't believe that anything outside of school is the business of the school. One
dean I knew thought it "unseemly" to plan for a student death, ration-
alizing that any planning would undermine the authenticity of feelings
generated "if and when" a student died. A number of principals with
whom I've worked were uncomfortable with "undue emotionality"
among students (how much is due?) and preferred instead to continue
with normal routine in the face of a nonroutine event. Some school
leaders feel that the grief generated by a student death is an individual
or family matter and should not concern the school group itself. These
leaders do not accept the concept or reality of group survivorship.

In contrast, why would group leaders naturally want to plan for a
death emergency? If the statistics Dr. Oates provides do not convince
the powers-that-be of their school community's vulnerability to a student or staff death and the need for proactive planning, then an honest
review of the emotional consequences of past losses should. In my
own classes on death, dying, and grief taught at the college level, I
have heard numerous accounts of how secondary schools have handled
a member's death. Students may report, "Oh, my high school didn't
care when Jimmy died in that accident. We went on as if nothing
happened." Or they may describe, with genuine pride, how their school
caringly stopped to recognize the death of a classmate. My question
to school leaders following the death of a group member is, "How will
students complete the following sentence: 'When my classmate died,
my school . . . .' "

An organized response to a member death is a statement of insti-
tutional caring for all surviving members. It is an indirect contract that
implies "this is what we would do for you should you die." And by sup-
porting directly group survivors who are most bereaved by the death,
all members are reassured that their organization does not count its
students, faculty, or staff as just names on the rolls.

Assuming that schools, as organized groups, do have concern for
the welfare of their members, that a member death affects group members negatively, and that an organized group response is perceived and
received as support of the entire group, the American Counseling As-

sociation has wisely seen the need to publish this book. Martha Oates has given us a "scholarly yet practical resource" to assist professionals in planning for the inevitable disruption of normal routine when a school member dies. She has succeeded admirably in providing a template with which any school community may prepare an appropriate and caring response to significant group loss. Of particular value are the checklists and charts that will help the reader evaluate the impact of a loss on the group and will prevent important details from being overlooked in the frenzy of the initial days following a crisis. For school systems that are now organizing their policies toward crisis intervention, the bibliography Dr. Oates provides will be most helpful.

At one point in this book, Dr. Oates describes a particular group ritual in a case example where the principal calls for a "corporate moment of silence in memory of the deceased." I was struck by the poignancy of the term, "corporate moment"—a designated moment in time shared by all members of a unified group. How a group responds to a member's death is perhaps the clearest indication of the value and respect afforded each *living* member of a group. Surely, our school communities pride themselves as organizations that go beyond the immediate goals of reading, writing, and arithmetic to promote the social and personal growth of each of its members. A relevant and sensitive response to the needs of the group during a time of crisis enhances both the individual and the group.

—*Ellen S. Zinner, PsyD*
Past President (1991–92)
Association for Death Education
and Counseling
Hartford, Connecticut

Preface

When a death occurs in the school community, all students, teachers, and staff are affected to some degree. In the case of a violent or sudden death, a school community may be deeply affected. Depending on how the school responds, the wide range of emotions and behaviors students exhibit can cause campuswide disruptions. Because the number of violent deaths involving children of all ages is growing, it is important that schools plan carefully how they will respond. The purpose of this book, *Death in the School Community: A Handbook for Counselors, Teachers, and Administrators*, is to assist schools to plan and respond effectively to a death.

According to recent government studies (National Center for Health Statistics [NCHS], 1992), there are 26.6 deaths per 100,000 annually among children 5 to 14 years of age and 87.4 per 100,000 among high school-age youths. One researcher (Atkinson, 1980) wrote that "by the age of 18, 1 child in 20 will have lost a parent by death, and in a school of 600 children, 1 child can be expected to die every second or third year" (p. 150). Increasing numbers of these deaths are violent. *Murder and suicide now alternate between second and third as the leading causes of death among high school students.* All of these deaths potentially affect thousands of classmates and teachers. The question no longer is *if* there will be a death that affects a school community, but *when*.

Seven years ago, I was one of three counselors at a new high school in suburban San Antonio, Texas. Although I had been a school counselor for 20 years, neither I, nor anyone else at this school, was prepared for the campuswide trauma that followed the suicide of a well-known student and the sudden death by natural causes of a young, popular teacher. When I was selected by the principal to plan the school's response after the student suicide, I searched extensively for ideas, plans, and materials that would guide our actions. I found almost no help in available publications or from discussions with other counselors and administrators. Some of the literature on grief recovery theory did provide useful information, and with that and my own knowledge of helping strategies, I devised our response plan. The plan proved effective and has been used, with only minor changes, after subsequent deaths that affected our school. Other educators, who have used elements of this plan with students of all ages, also report favorable results.

For the past 6 years, I have researched grief reactions in school-age children, crisis intervention techniques, and plans for responding to deaths that affect a school community. Based on my early research, I refined the school response plan and developed a workshop to train other professionals. Since 1987, over 800 counselors, teachers, and administrators have participated in this workshop—"Responding to Death in the Schools." Feedback from participants has been overwhelmingly positive. Most report that their graduate studies neither prepared them to assist grieving students nor encouraged planning for deaths that affect a school. Some of these educators had searched the literature for practical assistance when confronted with a death, but found a paucity of useful information. These experiences and my research indicated a need for a publication that would be a scholarly, yet practical resource. This handbook, based on my personal experience with grieving students and study of crisis intervention techniques and grief recovery theory, fulfills this need.

Death in the School Community will interest and provide useful information for school counselors, teachers, administrators, school safety officers, and crisis intervention specialists. Death educators, college professors, and practicum supervisors who train educators and counselors, and other professionals (e.g., social workers, hospital chaplains, psychologists, mental health and pastoral counselors, church youth leaders, and hospice workers) whose clients have death-related concerns will also find information they can use. This publication, with its discussions of research and theory, reports of effective practices, outlines for counseling groups, practical planning guides, and case studies, explains in detail how to plan for and respond to deaths that affect a school community. Readers will learn the importance of establishing a plan and learning strategies and techniques to facilitate healthy resolution of students' grief before a tragic event occurs. The focus of this publication is on death in elementary and secondary schools. It addresses specific needs of school personnel; however, much of the information can be adapted for use in other settings and with college students or older adults.

Chapter 1, "Death in the School Community: An Overview," shows the problem to be widespread and examines recent increases in the number of violent deaths. To provide a current perspective that addresses the rapid escalation of violent deaths among school-age children and youth, this book cites incidents reported in newspapers and news magazines over the past 12 months. Data from national studies and anecdotal evidence of homicides, suicides, accidental deaths, and deaths that occur *on* school campuses dramatize the need for response plans. Information in this chapter will increase the awareness level and knowledge base of school administrators, crisis intervention specialists, safety officers, counselors, teachers, and public information specialists. School officials will find data they can use to convince complacent colleagues that a tragic event can occur in their school community. Journalists who report school-related events and private practitioners who consult with school districts will also find this information useful.

In chapter 2, "Planning for Death in the School Community," the elements of an effective response plan are discussed, and a schema for determining the degree of campuswide trauma schools can expect from a particular death is presented. Determining the degree of trauma is important because these data affect the type of response the school staff will choose. This chapter addresses the duties of a planning task force and provides a detailed "action checklist" for use when widespread grief reactions are expected. The information will be of particular interest to campus administrators, safety officers, and crisis intervention specialists. The step-by-step guidelines will assist those who are inexperienced in responding to campuswide trauma following a death.

Planning appropriate responses requires an understanding of how students react to death. In chapter 3, "Understanding Grief in School-Age Children and Youth," common grief reactions of preschool through high school-age students related to particular deaths (e.g., those of parents, siblings, grandparents, and friends) are described. Because some students develop posttraumatic stress disorder (PTSD) after violent deaths, information is presented to assist school staff in identifying students who may be traumatized and need to be referred for professional counseling. Letters, essays, and poems written by students are included to help adults learn about grief from a child's perspective. Many techniques and strategies counselors and teachers can use to educate students about death and to facilitate healthy grief responses are described in chapter 4, "Facilitating Healthy Grief Responses." These include classroom guidance units, writing activities, artwork, memorials, puppetry, sand tray work, bibliotherapy, metaphors, and storytelling. Chapters 3 and 4 will increase the knowledge base and expand the repertoire of helping strategies that teachers, counselors, and other professionals (e.g., social workers, mental health and pastoral counselors, psychologists, and hospice workers) can use with the bereaved.

Chapter 5, "Leading Loss and Grief Groups," provides detailed information on group counseling with students after a death affects students campuswide as well as with students for whom the death is personal. The logistics of leading groups in a school setting—gaining administrative support, scheduling sessions, selecting group members, and notifying teachers—is addressed. Advocates of proactive, developmental guidance programs encourage schools to offer grief support groups routinely, not only in the aftermath of a tragedy. Schools are better prepared to respond when a tragic death occurs if they have support groups in place and their counselors and teachers are experienced in helping the bereaved. Included in this chapter are guides for group sessions relating to student suicides, other types of student deaths, and the death of a teacher. A detailed outline for an eight-session support group is also included. These guides were developed for use with students, but social workers, pastoral counselors, college counselors or student personnel specialists, mental health counselors, and hospice workers may find them useful in other settings and with college students or older adults.

Chapter 6, "Case Studies," illustrates the application of principles and strategies discussed in previous chapters and gives the reader opportunities to practice planning effective responses. All cases are based on actual events, but identifying data in some instances have been altered to provide confidentiality. Because few examples of deaths that affect the school community are available in professional literature, a number of the case studies were developed from news stories or the personal experiences of other professionals. Four cases—two student suicides (one in which gang rivalry was an issue), the death of a student in an automobile accident, and the homicide of a popular teacher—are presented in detail. Ten abbreviated cases with questions designed to stimulate the reader to think about appropriate responses are also included.

One case, the suicide of a student at the high school where I am a counselor, describes our school's *first* attempt 6 years ago at responding effectively. It does not, therefore, represent a textbook-perfect response. For example, we did not announce the name of the student who died (although everyone knew), much less mention that he had committed suicide! (In announcing subsequent deaths at our school, including suicides, we have stated very clearly the facts of the death. See sample announcements in Appendix B.) Because school officials failed to recognize the widespread impact of this death, we had to meet in the auditorium with 400 grieving students who came for help. Although this meeting went reasonably well, I do not recommend sharing information and processing feelings in a large group. A number of rooms to which students may go for small group counseling should be available when a death affects a campus.

The case of a student killed in an automobile accident involved a student at this same high school. The other student suicide and the teacher homicide were reported to me by crisis intervention specialists in the two school districts where these deaths occurred. The actions described in these three cases provide examples of effective response plans and can serve as guides for other schools when a similar death occurs. Information in this chapter will interest many people including school counselors, teachers, crisis intervention specialists, and administrators; college professors and practicum instructors who train educators and counselors; and mental health professionals who consult with schools. The cases in this chapter can be used as training aids with practicum students, counselor-trainees, and administrative interns, or as a means to consolidate the knowledge of experienced professionals.

The reference section, which lists all works cited, will be valuable to readers who want in-depth information on selected topics or who plan further research. The publication has two useful appendices. Appendix A is an annotated bibliography of books, articles, and other resources with sections titled "Loss and Grief Theory and Helping Strategies," "Crisis Management Planning," "Books for Children and Adolescents," and "Other Resources." Appendix B includes examples of memoranda related to response plans and sample forms for implementing grief support groups.

Although planning for a death that affects the school community may seem ghoulish, planning is important, indeed necessary, if educators are to help the bereaved while maintaining an effective learning climate in the school. Careful planning before a crisis occurs and informed, competent staff are essential components for an orderly resolution of the trauma that follows some deaths. Counselors, administrators, and teachers all have important roles to play, and this handbook can guide their actions. *Death in the School Community* provides the information I needed 6 years ago!

—*Martha D. Oates*
San Antonio, Texas
May, 1992

Acknowledgments

No individual develops or thrives in a vacuum, and the same is true of a publication. Therefore, I want to acknowledge some of the special people who have supported me and the development of this book.

I especially appreciate the support given to my work with grieving students and to the developmental guidance program at William Howard Taft High School by my principal, Roger W. Harris. I am also indebted to the many grieving students at this school who have shared intimately with me over the past 7 years and from whom I have learned much of what I know about responding effectively. The knowledge I gained from these experiences was the initial catalyst for this book.

I want to thank my good friend and colleague Eve Reed for reading a preliminary draft of this book and offering helpful suggestions related to clarity and mechanics. I am indebted to Mrs. Janice S. Gallagher, Director of Research and Developmental Programs, Harlandale Independent School District, and Dr. Betty Phillips, Coordinator, Office of Student Intervention Services, Austin Independent School District, for sharing ideas and materials from their crisis intervention experiences. They each supplied information for a detailed case study included in chapter 6. Dr. Phillips read a final draft of the book and made valuable observations as did Dr. Marjorie Cuthbert, Supervisor of Guidance and School Support Services, School Board of Alachua County. I must also thank Elaine Pirrone, my editor at the American Counseling Association, for patiently guiding a novice author.

I am grateful to my professors and colleagues Drs. Paul Johnson, John McQuary, and Harold Murphy of the Department of Counseling and Guidance at East Texas State University, Commerce, Texas, for nurturing my professional development over three decades. And, for his love and support, I wish to thank my life partner of 32 years, Dr. Arnold D. Oates, who has truly been "the wind beneath my wings" these past 12 months. Neither I, nor this publication, would have survived without his help!

About the Author

Martha D. Oates is a counselor at William Howard Taft High School in the Northside Independent School District, San Antonio, Texas, and a part-time instructor of group theory and process at the University of Texas at San Antonio. She is an active workshop presenter for students, parents, and professionals on loss and grief management, death in the schools, teenage suicide, group counseling techniques, assertiveness, stress management, and effective communication. Dr. Oates is a member of the American Counseling Association, and the Association for Death Education and Counseling and secretary of the Texas Counseling Association. She wrote the feature article, *"Reponding to Death in the Schools,"* for the Fall, 1988, issue of the *TACD Journal.*

Dr. Oates has lived and worked in several states, including Texas, Virginia, Oklahoma, Pennsylvania, California, and Maryland. She has been a French and English teacher, a middle and high school counselor, a guidance director, a community college counselor and administrator, and a part-time therapist at a community counseling center and a U.S. Department of Transportation program for alcohol abusers. Martha D. Oates is a Licensed Professional Counselor (LPC) and a National Certified Counselor (NCC). She received a bachelor of arts degree in English and master of education and doctor of education degrees in counseling from East Texas State University, Commerce, Texas, and has completed additional graduate study at the University of Virginia, The University of Richmond, Virginia Commonwealth University, and the University of North Texas. She is married and has two adult children, Katherine Cernosek and Marcus Oates.

CHAPTER 1

Death in the School Community:
An Overview

Violence has walked off the movie screen into real life. Kids don't have to buy a ticket anymore to see savagery played out in Central Texas. (Ward, 1991)

A newspaper reporter made the observation quoted above in an article about four teenage girls who were murdered during the robbery of a local yogurt shop. The reporter cited other recent acts of violence including four shootings at school buses, a shooting by police of a 14-year-old student on a school campus (when he rushed the officers with a weapon), and the stabbing death of a 13-year-old girl by a boy of the same age. These events were traumatic for the students and teachers at the schools the young victims attended (Ward,1991). Less than a month before, reporters for *The Orlando Sentinel* detailed escalating acts of violence in two Florida school districts under the headline "Reading, Writing—and Violence" (1991). In the 1990–91 school year, law enforcement officials made 417 arrests at Orange County, Florida, middle and high schools, compared with 221 in 1989–90. In nearby Seminole County, 131 students were arrested in 1990–91 for trespassing, assault, and weapons possession on campus, compared with only 80 the year before.

Although these reporters have regional perspectives, savagery and violence in the lives of school-age children are not relegated to any one state or area of the country, nor to a particular size of a town or a city. For example, in September 1991, residents of a small East Texas town with a population of less than 2,000 were shocked when a female student killed a male classmate with a handgun in the high school cafeteria. Parents and students in this community had believed that such acts of violence happened only in large cities. Unfortunately, in large cities like Chicago, Los Angeles, and New York, violence in schools occurs frequently. For example, according to the United Federation of Teachers, there were "16 students shot and 6 killed; 5 teachers shot and 1 killed; and 2 parents and 1 police officer shot" in the New York City public schools from September 1991 through early March 1992 (Flax, 1992, p. 22).

National studies show that young people are both the victims and the perpetrators of violent deaths nationwide. From 1980 through 1989, high school-age youths committed 11,000 homicides using firearms, cutting instruments, or blunt objects (Centers for Disease Control [CDC], October 11, 1991). One recent study (Lawton, 1991, p. 14) found that "the rate of Americans ages 15 to 19 killed by firearms increased by 43 percent between 1984 and 1988, to a record 17.7 deaths per 100,000 youths." Another study of students in grades 8 and 10 showed that "an estimated 135,000 boys nationwide in 1987 brought a gun to school daily" (Lawton, p. 14).

Murder and suicide alternate between second and third in a list of the leading causes of death among high school students, exceeded only by accidents (Office of Educational Research and Improvement [OERI], 1991). Seventy-five percent of the accidental deaths are caused by motor vehicle accidents. An estimated 4,000 school-age youths die in motor vehicle accidents each year, another 4,000 are murdered, and 3,800 kill themselves (CDC, March 22, 1991; OERI, 1991). The number of deaths related to gang involvement continues to grow, and according to research reported by Bodinger-deUriarte (1991), a new area of potential violence—hate crime—"has become a serious problem among the young and in the schools" (p. 1). U.S. Department of Justice data show that between 1986 and 1987, school-related racial incidents rose by almost 50%, pointing to a need for schools "to adopt policies, develop curriculum, and implement programs designed to prevent and curtail hate crime" (p. 5).

DEATH IN THE SCHOOL COMMUNITY IS NOT NEW

Although violent deaths are a recent phenomenon, deaths that affect the school community have occurred since the days of the one-room schoolhouse. Until recently, however, school officials usually ignored deaths or dealt with them in a matter-of-fact manner. Stanford (1977a) reported a typical incident:

> A junior high school student, who had been out of school more than a month with a fatal illness, died . . . . No official acknowledgement of the death was made at school the next day, nor the next week, nor ever thereafter. "It's just as though he disappeared," one of the boy's friends said. "No one ever made an announcement about it. I guess they thought we shouldn't know about it." (p. 308)

Ignoring a death in the school community may have been appropriate in an era when youth had more exposure to death and dying. In a discussion of children's concepts of death, Jozefowski (1983) observed that in earlier times "medical knowledge and sophisticated medical technology were limited. The mortality rates were high and most people died at home. Death was not a mystery, nor a taboo experience to the growing child" (p. 251). Today, however, increased geographic mobility separates children from older relatives, and more people die in hospital intensive care units than at home. These two aspects of contemporary life—mobility and modern medicine—have removed healthy exposure to death and dying from the lives of most children.

Although children view death almost daily in the unreality of television or movies, most are insulated from "real" death (Wass, Raup, & Sisler, 1989). Unfortunately, children who live in inner-city neighborhoods are frequently exposed to real violence and death. In a University of Alabama study conducted in the summer of 1991, 43% of the inner-city children ages 7 to 19 interviewed said they had witnessed a homicide ("It's Not Just," 1992, p. 29). A few years ago, an elementary school in the Watts area of Los Angeles instituted a loss and grief program in several classrooms because many students knew someone who had been murdered (Doherty, 1989). The death of a relative, neighbor, classmate, or teacher shatters children's illusions of invulnerability and immortality. Grieving students suffer varying degrees of distress, which can impair their ability to cope with normal school tasks.

SUICIDE AND HOMICIDE
AMONG OLDER YOUTHS

Disease accounts for less than one third of all deaths among individuals ages 5 to 24 and is no longer a major factor in the deaths of school-age children or younger teachers (U.S. Bureau of the Census, 1991, pp. 80–81). Today, most deaths among older youths are violent, and violent deaths cause traumatic grief reactions that affect a large portion of the school community. As stated earlier, suicide alternates with homicide as the second and third leading cause of death among all youth 15 to 19 years of age. The homicide death rate among high school-age youth in 1989 (the most recent year for which these data are available) was 13.7 per 100,000, up from 4.0 per 100,000 in 1960. *For minority young men in this age bracket, homicide is the number one cause of death,* with a rate of 75.7 per 100,000 (NCHS, 1992). The violent death rate for Black teenagers increased by 51% between 1984 and 1988, and for young men 15 to 19 years old, the homicide death rate reached an all-time high in 1989 of 92.7 per 100,000 (NCHS, 1992; Center for the Study of Social Policy, 1991).

The suicide rate for all youths 15 to 19 years of age has increased dramatically since 1960, when it was 5.3 per 100,000 for young men and 1.6 per 100,000 for young women. Depending on which data are examined, the current suicide rate is 17 to 19 per 100,000 for young men and 3 to 4 per 100,000 for young women, but rates vary considerably by race. White male teenagers, for example, with a rate of 19.6 per 100,000, are most prone to take their lives. Suicide rates among minority youth are lower, averaging 11.0 per 100,000 for young men and 2.6 for young women. The suicide rate for all youths 15 to 19 years of age is between 11 and 12 per 100,000 (OERI, 1991). An estimated 276,000 high school students make suicide attempts each year, and although no death occurs, attempts can affect students and teachers significantly (CDC, September 20, 1991).

Most educators are painfully aware that teen suicide has not diminished, and even "cluster" suicides continue. In a 2-week period in January 1992, three well-known students at a high school in suburban Houston killed themselves, and several other students made suicide attempts ("Schools Add," 1992). Three high school boys in Sheridan, Arkansas, killed themselves in 2 days in the spring of 1990. One of the three shot himself in his history class. Preceding these three deaths, another 17-year-old classmate had taken his life about 6 weeks earlier ("Students Mourning,"1990). During 1989, in Santa Fe County, New Mexico, six youths who were 10 to 19 years of age committed suicide, four by gunshot, one by hanging, and one by motor vehicle exhaust fumes. When two high school boys killed themselves within a 4-day period the following February, school officials became alarmed. Their reports to the New Mexico Department of Health prompted a study, which revealed that 144 youths had attempted suicide in Santa Fe county in the past 5 years (CDC, May 24, 1991).

SUICIDE AMONG CHILDREN

Unfortunately suicides, murders, and violent accidents are not limited to the world of older youths. A National Adolescent Student Health Survey of 11,000 students in grades 8 to 12 showed that 34% of the eighth graders had thought seriously about suicide and 15% had made attempts (Herring, 1990). Barrett (1989) reported that suicide is the sixth leading cause of death for children ages 5 to 14. Stefanowski-Harding (1990) noted that although accidents are listed as the number one cause of death in children, "the Suicide Prevention Center of Los Angeles estimates that 50% of the deaths reported as accidents are, in fact, suicides" (p. 329). Frequently, it seems, the suicides of young children are hidden from public scrutiny. The National Center for Health Statistics (U.S. Bureau of the Census, 1991, p. 360) reported 140 confirmed cases of suicide in 1988 among children ages 5 to 14, but other sources (Herring) found estimates as high as 200 annually.

OTHER VIOLENT DEATHS

Murders of young children and accidental deaths involving firearms increased over the past decade (U.S. Bureau of the Census, 1991), and violent deaths among school-age children are reported almost daily in news stories. Headlines from the *San Antonio Express-News*, a daily newspaper in a southern city with a population of 900,000, are representative of those from across the nation. In one 6-month period in late 1991 and early 1992, headlines declared: "Three teens charged in fatal attack on 14-year-old boy"; "Boy, 12, found guilty of murder"; "Siblings, 8 and 12, gunned down as mom showers"; "14-year-old shot dead in street clash"; "Freshman kills self at high school"; "Teen gang crashes birthday party; girl killed, 8 injured"; "Girl shoots self on school grounds"; "Teen says he shot 3 youths, killed 1 in self-defense"; "Shot from auto kills 14-year-old"; and "Driver of fleeing car charged in death of girl, 8." The stories behind these headlines underscore the need for schools to develop effective response plans. When students die violently, the impact on the school community can be profound.

On a Saturday in May 1990, a 14-year-old middle school student burned to death in a small building behind his home in a fire that investigators ruled arson. The boy, who was to testify in court on Monday in an assault case, had told a friend that he feared for his life (Edwards, 1990). Anticipating that grief reactions at the local middle school would be severe, the school district's crisis team implemented their response plan. This young man was 1 of 16 children ages 15 and younger murdered in that city in 1990.

In midafternoon in the summer of 1991, a 12-year-old boy and a 15-year-old friend were playing with a pellet rifle at the older boy's suburban home. The gun accidentally discharged, and the younger boy was killed by a pellet that struck him in the chest. Because school was in summer recess when the death occurred, the impact on this student's school was not as severe (when school resumed for the fall term) as it might have been. However, some students, including the sister of the boy who died, sought counseling. The school counselor referred the older boy and his mother to a community mental health agency for in-depth counseling.

In December 1991, a 14-year-old boy left his aunt's home located in an inner-city area of a large South Texas city at 11:30 P.M. As he walked to a nearby pay phone to call for a ride home, four youths approached and demanded to know to what gang he belonged. When he answered, "None," they beat him with baseball bats and shot him several times. He died before medical assistance arrived ("Gang Members," 1991).

At 12:50 A.M. on a Sunday morning in February 1992, an eighth-grade girl was killed and eight other people injured when several teen-agers came to the door and fired randomly into a house located in a quiet neighborhood (Edwards, 1992). The incident happened at the home of a middle school student whose parents were hosting a party in honor of her 14th birthday. According to news reports, the teenagers who fired the shots were looking for rival gang members. The girl who died was a middle school honor student and member of the soccer team. Several of the wounded students attended the same middle school. Grief reactions were severe both in the school and surrounding community.

DEATHS ON THE SCHOOL CAMPUS

Although school accidents that cause deaths are rare, crimes on campus have increased dramatically in the past 5 years. A recent U.S. Department of Justice survey "found that 2 percent of students—or an estimated 400,000—had been the victims of a violent crime at school" (Lawton, 1991, p. 14). A study by the Center to Prevent Handgun Violence (1990), based solely on newspaper reports, found that from September 1986 to September 1990, at least 65 students and 6 school employees were killed with guns on school campuses across the nation. Another 201 individuals were wounded severely, and 242 were held hostage at gunpoint. (These numbers do not include similar incidents in which weapons other than guns were used.) Although the majority, 63%, of these gun-related incidents occurred on high school campuses, 37% were at junior high and elementary schools. According to the study, the most common places for campus shootings were hallways (between class periods) and classrooms. Following violent deaths, many students and staff may exhibit fear and anger in addition to grief. When deaths occur on the school campus, whether due to disastrous accidents or criminal acts, the school's immediate and long-term responses need to be especially well planned.

On November 10, 1976, a man walked into a second-grade classroom in Detroit, Michigan, argued with the teacher, pulled out a revolver, and shot her several times in full view of 30 students. The confusion following the incident, as police cars with flashing lights and sirens arrived, added to the students' trauma. Bruce Danto (1978), the psychologist who coordinated the school's response, described the immediate and long-term measures taken following this tragic event.

He met many times with staff, parents, and students and employed special strategies to prepare those who testified in court. Danto observed that "the children were not the only ones traumatized—we also found that the parents were overwhelmed with anxiety . . . . The children who did not cope well had parents who did not cope well" (p. 88). Parents felt guilty that they could not protect their children from this tragedy. In addition to meeting the needs of teachers and students, the school staff must consider how parents and the larger community are affected.

In September 1988, a man carrying a handgun entered an elementary school in Greenwood, South Carolina, walked to the cafeteria, and began to shoot. Three first-grade students and one teacher were injured by the gunfire. The man reloaded his gun, entered a third-grade classroom, and fired again, fatally wounding two students. Panicked students in this section of the building scampered outside and ran to the nearby woods. In addition to the two deaths, seven students and two teachers were wounded in this incident. The school was closed for 2 days following the shooting. The building needed to be cleaned and repaired, and teachers and staff needed time to deal with their own feelings of sadness, guilt, and fear. Watson, Poda, Miller, Rice, and West (1990) reported that "the teachers were confused and horrified. They did not feel safe. They were not ready to help students feel safe" (p. 4). Parents questioned the ability of the school to protect their children from harm. District staff employed several strategies, including an open house at the school, to regain community confidence and reassure parents and students that the school was a safe place.

In January 1989, a gunman with an AK-47 automatic rifle opened fire on 400–500 children on the playground of an elementary school in Stockton, California. He killed 5 children and wounded 30 others. The resulting trauma both within the school and in the community was severe. More than 50 social workers, school psychologists, public health nurses, other health professionals, and interpreters responded immediately. They counseled students, school staff, parents, law enforcement officers, rescue workers, and medical personnel who treated the children. Because this was a culturally diverse community, officials established a 24-hour hotline in five languages and placed interpreters in the school and local counseling centers. Despite its efforts to be culturally sensitive, the school district was criticized by a Vietnamese social worker for opening the school the day after the tragedy. Hiratsuka (1989) reported that some professionals "questioned the effectiveness of Western-style crisis counseling for Southeast Asian families with ugly memories of wars and refugee camps" (p. 9).

On April 4, 1991, an airplane carrying a U.S. senator collided in midair with a helicopter and crashed onto the grounds of an elementary school in the Lower Merion (Pennsylvania) School District. Two first-grade girls were killed and three other children and two adults were injured by burning debris. Emergency medical service personnel and police responded quickly, but the school's telephone lines were overloaded with calls from parents and others wanting information or offering assistance. Students at the school and citizens in the community were devastated by this extraordinary event. The district's crisis team set up telephone hotlines and established a drop-in counseling center in the community. The supervisor of guidance services noted that because a crisis intervention network was already in place, the school district and community could respond quickly and effectively (Modrak, 1992, p. 4).

In September 1991, the captain of the varsity football team at Crosby High School was shot and killed in the school cafeteria by a female student who shouted, "You called me a bitch!" Shots from her .38-caliber revolver sent other students, who were eating breakfast, scurrying for cover. Residents in this small East Texas town of 1,811 were horrified that violence had invaded their quiet community, much less its schools. They believed that these things happened only in big cities ("It's Not Just," 1992, p. 25).

On Friday, May 1, 1992, a disgruntled former student, armed with several weapons including a 12-gauge shotgun, held more than 75 individuals hostage on the campus of a central California high school (Sommerfeld, 1992a). The 20-year-old entered the school about 2:00 P.M. and went from classroom to classroom firing at students randomly. When the emotional ordeal ended 8 hours later, three students and a 28-year-old teacher were dead and nine others were injured, some critically. The students, their families, and other residents in this agricultural community near Olivehurst, California, were stunned by these senseless acts of violence.

Each of the incidents described above shattered the illusion that such a tragedy "could never happen in our school or community." Children who are murdered, like those who take their lives, come from all socioeconomic levels and from every type of community. These tragic accidents and violent crimes on school campuses dramatize the need for effective response plans.

RESPONSE PLANS

Formalized plans for responding to death in the school community were rarely found before the late 1970s, and most of the early plans resulted from the rising incidence of youth suicide (Barrett, 1989). By mid-1980, however, a growing number of educators recognized the need for comprehensive plans. Articles appeared in professional journals detailing responses to specific incidents or promoting crisis planning. Some educators (Hunt, 1987; Pelej, 1987) wrote about their districts' responses to student suicides and recommended elements of an effective crisis plan. Palmo, Langlois, and Bender (1988) discussed legal implications; the role of the school board, staff, and teachers; and guidelines to follow in the event of a student suicide. In *How to Handle Death in the School*, the National Association of Secondary School Principals (1986) suggested that plans be developed for different types of deaths, including students killed in auto accidents, the death of siblings, and national tragedies such as the space shuttle explosion.

Counselors wrote about effective plans and their role in assisting grieving students. Zinner (1987) reported the steps taken after an elementary student killed himself, and Oates (1988) described in detail the strategies used after the sudden death (by natural causes) of a young, popular high school teacher. Arena, Hermann, and Hoffman (1984) wrote about effective responses to student trauma after the brutal murder of an elementary school classmate. Collison et al. (1987) described the actions taken after a middle school principal was killed in the hallway by a 14-year-old armed with several guns. Although the school district did not have a crisis plan, some of the actions taken after this death were effective; others were not. Collison asked pointedly: "If there is an incident in your school, will you have a plan developed to respond . . . or will you, at a time of extreme confusion and stress, have to improvise on the spot?" (p. 65).

Despite these articles and the increasing publicity given to deaths that affect schools, many districts and individual school campuses have no plan, or have only general guidelines, for meeting the needs of their students, faculty, and larger school community. Mortality statistics for school-age children and news stories about such deaths underscore the importance of having a response plan. Recent data report 26.6 deaths per 100,000 annually among children 5 to 14 years of age and 87.4 per 100,000 among high school youths (NCHS, 1992; OERI, 1991). These deaths affect thousands of classmates and teachers.

SUMMARY

Very few secondary schools have escaped the tragedy of student suicide and the ensuing impact on the school community. Violent deaths, both accidental and intentional, also are affecting children of all ages in increasing numbers. Schools that have not experienced a tragic death probably will in the future. It is no longer a question of *if* there will be a death that affects a school campus, but rather *when*. These deaths, even when not violent in nature, can affect the school community deeply. Simply ignoring a death or dealing with it in a matter-of-fact manner will not accomplish the goal of being helpful to those who are grieving while maintaining an effective learning climate in the school. The needs of students, teachers, staff, and parents must all be considered. Careful planning before a crisis and informed, competent staff are essential for an orderly resolution of trauma after a death affects the school community. Administrators, counselors, and teachers all have a role to play in ensuring that their school will be prepared to respond effectively. Chapter 2 provides information and guidelines to assist those who are charged with developing a response plan.

CHAPTER 2

Planning for Death in the School Community

The death of a student or staff in a given school is a significant stress and/or loss event to those persons in that system. It impacts individuals as well as the educational process itself. . . [and] observation and logic reveals that academic performance wanes when students and staff are questioning the "whys" and "hows" surrounding the death of a fellow school person. ("At-Risk," 1991)

The process of responding effectively when a death affects the school community has many steps. Some require leadership and direction from the district office, but most are implemented by the school principal and others at the local campus. Because teachers and counselors work directly with students, they implement or provide input for many steps. Being prepared to respond to all types of emergencies that may occur is important; however, the scope of this book is limited to *death* as a particular type of crisis in the school community. The focus is on planning responses that will return the campus to normalcy as quickly as possible.

DEVELOPING A PLAN

School districts without a systemwide crisis management plan, or written policies to give direction to individual campuses, should develop these as a first step. Typically, the district superintendent or designated staff members develop a districtwide plan for approval by the district's governing board (e.g., the board of education). Central office leaders can study crisis plans and policies from other districts with similar demographics before developing their district's plan. A list of districts willing to share information can be secured from professional associations that serve school boards and administrators. Three recent publications, *At-Risk Youth in Crisis* (1991); *School Crisis Survival Guide* (Petersen & Straub, 1992); and *Containing Crisis* (Watson et al.,1990) provide detailed information about responding to deaths and developing crisis management plans. The National School Safety Center, located in Westlake Village, California, and the Program in Trauma, Violence, and Sudden Bereavement at the University of California at Los Angeles have provided assistance to schools following violent deaths (Sommerfeld, 1992b).

As noted earlier, many districts and individual schools do not have a crisis response plan, or have one that addresses only a limited number of crises (e.g., weather disasters, campus fires, or suicides). Comprehensive plans offer specific steps to follow when a death, by whatever cause, affects the campus or when other crises (as remote as an armed intruder or an airplane crash) endanger students' lives. Each school campus should have a comprehensive plan tailored to its own special needs and available staff. The plan should be developed by campus personnel and community representatives appointed by the principal. One or more teachers, administrators, counselors and, if available, the school nurse, security officer, and community mental health professionals should serve on the planning task force. Palmo et al. (1988) stressed the need to build support among staff members when developing a crisis plan and to "be prepared to face the many who deny problems, argue that it is not the school's job, or claim that any focus on the problem will exacerbate it" (p. 101). Watson et al. (1990) and a Centers for Disease Control report (1988) emphasized the importance of including representatives from the news media, law enforcement agencies, fire department, civil defense agencies, and parents in the planning effort.

Task Force Duties

The work of the planning task force will be guided by goals the school principal sets, district policies, and the expertise of committee members. Duties of the task force should include the following:

1. Identify the types of deaths (e.g., student homicide, multiple deaths in an automobile accident, teacher dying at school) that might occur.
2. Solicit ideas about effective responses (for each type of death identified) from:
   - Other campus personnel;
   - Other schools;
   - Mental health and medical professionals;
   - Fire, police and emergency medical service officials; and
   - Professional publications, including ideas from this book. (Appendix A and the reference section list journal articles and books that may be useful.)

3. Consider effective responses and determine those appropriate for this campus.
4. Identify individuals within the school and community who can perform specific tasks needed to implement the plan.
5. Prepare a detailed plan to present to the principal for approval.

Oates (1988) suggested that the planning committee consider these questions when devising a plan for responding to a death:

1. Who will be the one and only spokesperson (e.g., a campus-based person or a central office media aide) for the school in the event of a death?
2. Who will notify the next of kin if a death occurs at school?
3. Who will be responsible for removing personal effects of the deceased from the classroom and/or locker?
4. How will staff and students be informed?
5. What classroom activities, if any, related to a particular death are appropriate?
6. What will be the policy concerning attendance at a funeral held on a school day? Is a campus memorial service warranted?
7. Who will provide for the emotional needs of students and staff following announcement of the death?
8. Do these providers need additional training?
9. Who will be responsible for training the staff to carry out the response plan?
10. How will the plan be evaluated? (pp. 86–87)

Subcommittees may be used to develop specific aspects of the plan, for example, planning in-service training of teachers, developing classroom units, procuring safety supplies, evaluating the school's communication system, preparing announcements, interfacing with community agencies, evaluating community mental health professionals who may be called in to assist school counselors, or developing a communication network.

Each campus develops subcommittees based on local needs and staff and assigns appropriate duties. For example, in some schools a subcommittee of teachers and counselors (rather than the task force as a whole) develops classroom activities or plans in-service programs for parents and staff. Another group is responsible for procuring, maintaining, and storing in an easily accessible place the equipment, supplies, and information needed if deaths occur on campus. These items may include first aid supplies and manuals, stretchers, portable bullhorns, lists of staff who know CPR, stick-on name tags and magic markers (for use in identifying victims), names and phone numbers of district and community personnel who can be contacted for assistance, floor plans of the building, and backup computer disks of enrollment data.

A communication subcommittee is especially useful on large campuses. This group establishes a *telephone tree* for relaying information to teachers and staff, organizes practice sessions using this method of communication, and evaluates the campus communication system to determine if it will be adequate in a major emergency. For example, is the intercom or public address system in good working order? What other means can be used to communicate on campus if the public address system is disabled in the crisis? Are there enough telephone trunk lines into the school to handle increased telephone traffic? Are there one or more lines into the school with unpublished numbers? In an emergency the telephone lines with *published* numbers may become jammed from the volume of calls. How will teachers be alerted if a violent intruder enters the building and poses a threat to the safety of students and staff? A special code message can be given over the public address system to alert teachers to lock classroom doors or take other precautions. For example, in a school that does not have a wrestling team, the principal might announce: *"The wrestling match scheduled for this afternoon has been canceled. Students and teachers please note, the wrestling match has been canceled."* The code should be changed periodically.

Elements of an Effective Plan

An effective plan for responding to a death that affects a school has three components: *prevention, intervention*, and *postvention*. **Prevention** measures may include the following:

- A functioning crisis management team that can be activated when a death occurs;
- Staff and teacher training on steps to follow if a death occurs on campus, how to evacuate students whose safety is endangered by a natural disaster or violent intruder, and what to take with them (e.g., roll book or attendance cards);
- Practice sessions related to locking classroom doors or evacuating the building for crises other than the usual fire drill;
- Training programs for staff and teachers on how to recognize students who are in crisis and how to assist grieving students;

- Student assistance programs (e.g., peer helpers; buddy system for new students; support groups for students);
- Wallet-sized cards (issued with school identification cards) giving phone numbers for local resources that students can call in times of crisis;
- Parent education programs on recognizing depression in children, understanding grief, and effective parent-child communication; and
- Curriculum units on death and dying.

Paying careful attention to prevention activities will ensure that intervention measures, when they are needed, proceed more smoothly. Although the actions discussed above are helpful in preparing for most deaths that affect a campus, *preventing* student suicides may require additional strategies. Many writers (Barrett, 1989; Capuzzi & Golden, 1988; Johnson & Maile, 1987; Pfeifer, 1986) have addressed in detail specific suicide prevention measures schools can implement.

Intervention, or immediate action, is based on the established crisis management plan. Once a death is known, the principal convenes the task force or crisis team to determine what parts of the plan will be implemented. The planned response will vary depending on the expected degree of trauma. (Determining the degree of trauma is discussed later in this chapter.)

The following checklist is designed for use when deaths occur that are expected to cause considerable campuswide trauma. If little or no campuswide trauma is expected, only a few of these steps will be needed. Appropriate actions depend on the nature of the death, when and where it occurred, the size of the district and the school, and the personnel available. In some instances the time and date each step is completed should be noted.

Action Checklist

_____ 1. The principal notifies the district's school superintendent or other designated central office staff person (unless notification of the death came from central office personnel).

_____ 2. The principal notifies the crisis team, key campus personnel, and appropriate central office personnel (e.g., student intervention coordinator, public information officer, or psychologist) of the death. The principal sets a time and place for these individuals to meet. Depending on the time available, this group may accomplish some or all of the following tasks:

- Meet individually or in small groups with teachers who will be personally affected by the death. Schedule a faculty meeting and notify all teachers and staff of the death and the time and place of the meeting.
- Arrange for substitutes for some teachers if warranted and advise them of the faculty meeting. Substitutes who are familiar with the school may serve as "rovers" to relieve any teacher who is grieving or needs a break.
- Prepare announcements to be read to students, a script for those who answer the school's telephones, and a press release for the media. In case of a suicide, a fact sheet concerning appropriate reporting of the death may be given to media representatives (Eisenberg, 1986).
- Prepare a memorandum for teachers (see Appendix B) including the announcement, suggestions for being helpful to students, sign-in logs for counseling rooms, and forms to list the names of students referred for counseling or who may need monitoring for adverse reactions to the death.
- Identify, especially after a student suicide or other violent death, the deceased student's close friends and other friendship groups (e.g., sports teams or clubs). Make contact with these students and/or their parents.
- Decide if any schoolwide events (e.g., standardized testing or athletic events) need to be canceled or rescheduled.
- Designate rooms and school staff for counseling grieving students after the death is announced. Decide if community mental health professionals are needed.
- Brief those who will provide the counseling.
- Designate school personnel to monitor halls during class changes and restrooms throughout the day.
- Develop a plan of action for crowd control, emotional contagion, or disruptive behavior in the event these occur.
- Determine if parent meetings are advisable and work with parent organizations to schedule these.
- Notify the principal and/or counselor at other schools where close relatives (i.e., children, siblings, or parents) of the deceased are enrolled or employed.

_____ 3. The principal, or other designated staff member, checks with appropriate authorities (e.g., police department or coroner's office) concerning the facts (who, when, how, and where) of the death before the crisis task force meets or as soon as possible. After a student suicide, it is advisable to secure parent permission before announcing the death. Do not characterize the death as a suicide until the cause of death is determined by the coroner's or medical examiner's office. (A coroner's decision is public information.)

_____ 4. The school principal contacts the deceased person's parents (or other next of kin) to offer condolences and to advise them of the school's planned response. (Note: Check local policy concerning flying a flag at half-mast following a death. Usually national and state flags are flown at half-mast only when approved by the appropriate governmental agency. School staff need to be aware that any actions they take may set a precedent.)

_____ 5a. **The school principal meets with all faculty and staff**, including support and classified employees, to inform them of the death and planned response. At the principal's discretion, representatives of parent organizations or community leaders may be invited to this meeting. Each teacher receives an announcement about the death to be read at a designated time (e.g., the first period of the day). This announcement usually *should not* be made over the public address system.

Faculty and staff are provided the name and phone number of the district's approved media spokesperson (i.e., the principal, district crisis coordinator, or public information officer) to whom they should refer all media requests. Interviews with this spokesperson should be held *away from the school campus* and efforts made to keep reporters from interviewing or filming students at the school. The principal announces the time of subsequent faculty meetings (for example, at the close of the school day).

_____ 5b. **If no faculty/staff meeting can be held**, a *telephone tree* or a detailed memorandum to all faculty and staff is used to communicate the death. It is important that faculty members be fully informed before they meet with their students. Each telephone-tree caller has accurate and identical information to relay.

_____ **6.** At the faculty meeting, the school counselor (or other mental health professional) gives suggestions for assisting distraught students and explains the logistics of sending students for counseling. The principal requests that all teachers report to a designated place (e.g., the counseling office) during their planning or conference period to offer assistance.

_____ **7a.** **Student death.** A counselor follows the deceased student's class schedule (in middle or high school) throughout the day or meets with the class of an elementary student to help classmates clarify their feelings and discuss concerns related to the death. A deceased student's desk *should not* be removed immediately.

_____ **7b.** **Teacher death.** An experienced teacher on the campus (not a substitute teacher) meets the deceased teacher's class(es) the following day, and perhaps for several days. A school counselor or other mental health professional is present the first day to help students process their feelings about the death.

_____ **8.** Volunteer counselors (from other schools or community agencies) sign in at a central location where they are provided name tags, maps of the school, and the teacher memorandum. Individuals who answer the school's telephones take information from callers who offer assistance. A designated staff person screens the information and approves all off-campus volunteers.

_____ **9.** A designated staff person removes personal effects of the deceased from classrooms and lockers. These items are screened and returned to the next of kin by a counselor, teacher, or the principal at a time convenient to the survivors. School staff follow local regulations concerning who may release suicide notes or written materials containing information about crimes or threats to others.

_____ **10.** Near the end of the school day, the principal uses the public address system to call for a corporate moment of silence in memory of the deceased. The principal gives information about the funeral (or where this information will be available) and encourages students who need further assistance to contact a teacher or counselor.

_____ **11.** The principal meets with faculty and staff at the end of the school day to assess the situation and receive feedback or suggestions concerning future actions. Counselors collect names of students who may need special

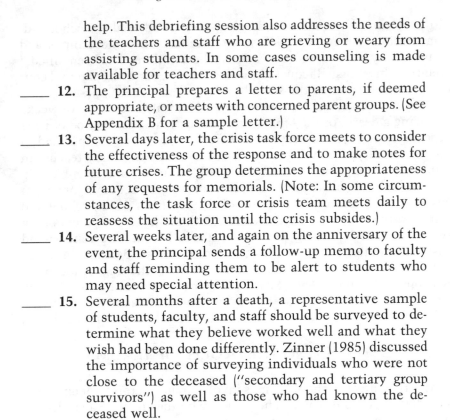

help. This debriefing session also addresses the needs of the teachers and staff who are grieving or weary from assisting students. In some cases counseling is made available for teachers and staff.

_____ 12. The principal prepares a letter to parents, if deemed appropriate, or meets with concerned parent groups. (See Appendix B for a sample letter.)

_____ 13. Several days later, the crisis task force meets to consider the effectiveness of the response and to make notes for future crises. The group determines the appropriateness of any requests for memorials. (Note: In some circumstances, the task force or crisis team meets daily to reassess the situation until the crisis subsides.)

_____ 14. Several weeks later, and again on the anniversary of the event, the principal sends a follow-up memo to faculty and staff reminding them to be alert to students who may need special attention.

_____ 15. Several months after a death, a representative sample of students, faculty, and staff should be surveyed to determine what they believe worked well and what they wish had been done differently. Zinner (1985) discussed the importance of surveying individuals who were not close to the deceased ("secondary and tertiary group survivors") as well as those who had known the deceased well.

The **postvention** or follow-up component of an effective plan should be proactive. The last three items on the previous checklist are examples of postvention actions. Other measures may include school-based loss and grief counseling groups as described in chapter 5, individual counseling, parent conferences, and referral of students to community mental health professionals. School counselors should consult with teachers concerning individual students who require monitoring for unhealthy grief reactions. In-service programs or counseling may be provided for the faculty and staff who were involved in meeting students' needs.

Parent group meetings, seminars, or other activities may be scheduled to address parent and community concerns. Input from parents and community patrons should be solicited and considered. Sometimes special situations call for special responses. After a violent incident on the school campus, an open house can help students and parents feel that the school is safe and secure. School personnel must be sensitive to students or parents from different cultures (Kalish & Reynolds, 1981). In the Stockton elementary schoolyard shooting "where many

of the victims were of Asian descent, parents advised the school ad-
ministration to have a Buddhist monk come onto the campus and
sprinkle holy water in those locations where children had been killed."
Granting this unusual request "was essential in restoring parental confidence and support in the school" (Watson et al., 1990, p. 46).

Postvention activities may be needed for only a few days or weeks
following a death, or they may continue for years. The period of time
depends on the type of death and degree of trauma on campus and in
the community. For example, the murder of an elementary teacher in
full view of her students and the death in an auto accident of six
popular high school students in a rural community required long-term
postvention measures. In the case of the teacher's death, school and
community counselors were involved with students and parents for a
year (Danto, 1978). The grief counselor who led the intervention and
postvention efforts after the high school students' deaths worked in
the school and community for 2 years following the tragedy (Schaefer
& Lyons, 1988, pp. 55–56). Special activities may need to be planned
for the anniversary date of a tragic event. Students, faculty, and parents
will be aware of this date, whether or not it is officially noted.

DETERMINING THE DEGREE OF TRAUMA

Deaths that affect a school campus involve many factors—for example,
who died, how, and where. The person who dies may be a student, a
teacher, an administrator, other school personnel, or a popular local
and national figure (e.g., a professional athlete). The cause of death
may be natural, accidental, suicide, or murder, and the death may be
unexpected or anticipated, as in the case of long-term illness. Deaths
may occur at school, in the local community, or far away. The "who,
how, and where" of the death determines the degree of trauma that is
likely to follow. Oates (1988) developed a schema (see Figure 1) to
determine the expected degree of trauma by assigning certain values
to specific details of the death:

> For example, if a student, not well known (assign a value of 3)
> takes his own life (6) at his home (2), a moderate degree of
> trauma (grand total of 11) will be evident. If a student who has
> only been in school for a few months (3) dies of an accidental
> gunshot wound (3) while visiting his grandparents in another
> city (1), the trauma evident in the student body will be low. By
> contrast, if a popular and well-known teacher (4) who is young
> (2) dies of natural, but unexplained causes (4) at her home in
> the community (2), a very high degree of trauma can be expected
> (grand total of 12). (p. 84)

Figure 1
Determining Expected Degree of Trauma

Step 1: Circle the number(s) in each triangle beside any word or phrase that describes this death. Total circled numbers within each triangle.

Step 2: Add triangle totals. Then add one point for each additional person who died or was critically injured in this event to determine a GRAND TOTAL: _____

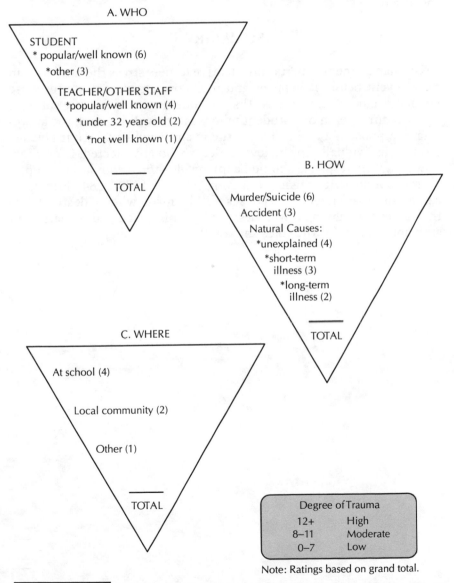

A. WHO

STUDENT
* popular/well known (6)

*other (3)

TEACHER/OTHER STAFF
*popular/well known (4)

*under 32 years old (2)

*not well known (1)

TOTAL

B. HOW

Murder/Suicide (6)

Accident (3)

Natural Causes:
*unexplained (4)

*short-term illness (3)

*long-term illness (2)

TOTAL

C. WHERE

At school (4)

Local community (2)

Other (1)

TOTAL

Degree of Trauma
12+   High
8–11   Moderate
0–7   Low

Note: Ratings based on grand total.

In using this schema, school personnel should add points for multiple deaths or injuries. Multiple deaths have the potential to cause greater trauma than single deaths. However, if the death occurs when school is not in session (during the summer months, for example), points may be subtracted from the total. Deaths that occur when school is not in session have a lesser impact on a campus than those that occur during the school year.

SUMMARY

Crisis management experts and effective leaders stress the need to plan for an event before it happens and to choose an appropriate response when it occurs. With some deaths (e.g., one that occurs in the summer or the natural death of a student who was not well known), the appropriate response may be to ignore the event campuswide, but give assistance individually to the few students who are affected. Even then, however, "the response should be 'planned'—*there should be a sound reason for choosing to ignore the event*" (Oates, 1988, p. 84). Principals can ensure that effective responses will be made when a death affects the campus by having a well-designed plan in place and preparing all staff and faculty for the roles they will play.

■ CHAPTER 3 ■

Understanding Grief in School-Age Children and Youth

*Simply put, grief is a normal and natural response to loss . . .
[but] grieving is the most misunderstood and neglected growth
process a person can go through. (James & Cherry, 1988)*

A s noted in chapter 1, the prevalence of death in the lives of school-age children is increasing, and the number of students identified as being *at-risk* grows each year. Meeting the needs of these students requires a large investment of time, money, and personnel and, therefore, affects a total school community. Disruptive behavior, school phobia, learning problems, and hyperactivity of some at-risk students are the result of unresolved grief (Jewett, 1982; Wolfelt, 1983). Drug and alcohol abuse, suicide, and delinquent behavior in children and youth have also been linked to grief reactions (Crenshaw, 1990; Markusen & Fulton, 1971; Moriarty, 1983), and incomplete recovery from loss can affect the capacity for happiness throughout one's lifetime (James & Cherry, 1988; Moriarty, 1983). Children who are disruptive in school or make suicide attempts are not only a risk to themselves, but affect the learning environment of all students. Helping grieving students has the potential to improve the school climate for all who work and learn there. To be effective helpers, however, educators must understand how children and adolescents react to loss in unique ways.

Many grief therapists and death education specialists (Bertoia & Allan, 1988; Bowlby, 1979; Crenshaw, 1990; Jewett, 1982; Wass & Corr, 1984a; Wolfelt, 1983) have studied children's understanding of death and their reactions to loss. Researchers have focused on grief reactions of preschoolers, elementary school children, and adolescents based on their developmental stage and their relationship to the person who died (e.g., parent, sibling, grandparent, classmate, or teacher). Information from these studies is summarized below. The books and articles listed in Appendix A provide in-depth information about grief in school-age children and their concepts of death.

CHILDREN'S GRIEF REACTIONS

Even very young children grieve losses, but their reactions differ somewhat from those of adults (Wass & Corr, 1984a). Because of their limited verbal ability, preschoolers often express grief by becoming physically ill, refusing to eat, becoming hyperactive, breaking things, or withdrawing emotionally. A young child may seem indifferent to the death of someone close, a family member, for example, and play happily at recess a short time after learning about the death. Teachers and counselors should not be misled by this behavior. Wolfelt (1983) observed that children go through a denial stage just as older grievers do, and showing indifference or lack of feeling protects the child from full acknowledgment of the death. Crenshaw (1990) found that children "feel deep sadness and longing and need to be encouraged to put these feelings into words. They may not be able to stay with these feelings for very long and, once having shared them, may feel a need to retreat and talk about other things" (p. 81). Children in the primary grades may resort to baby talk, cling to adults, startle easily, and wet or soil their pants. Teachers will need to be patient with young students who exhibit regressive behaviors following a death.

Children from 3 to 9 years of age engage in *magical thinking*; that is, they believe they are very powerful and that their thoughts and deeds make things happen (Jewett, 1982; Schaefer & Lyons, 1988). Most young children *want* to believe in magic, fairy tales, and superheroes. Wass (1984a) wrote that for young children "there are no random events. Everything is caused" (p. 7). It is not unusual for children to connect unrelated events. A grieving child, for example, may believe that his or her anger or spiteful actions toward the person who died actually caused the death. Even adolescents engage in a form of magical thinking when they believe that perhaps they could have prevented a death: *"If only I had told someone he was joking about killing himself." "If only I had been at home when Dad had his heart attack."* Tatelbaum (1980) suggested that "when we imagine that if we had acted differently we might have prevented the death, we figuratively endow ourselves with superhuman powers to change destiny" (p. 35).

Oates (1988) pointed out that conflicting emotions, including anger at the person who died, resentment of those who survive, or self-pity, "add to the difficulties young people have in processing their grief" (p. 89). Grieving students need to know that "anger at loss is normal and provides an outlet for the frustration and helplessness one feels." The knowledgeable counselor or teacher can help students "understand that a wide range of emotions, even these 'unacceptable' ones, are present in most who suffer a loss. Permission must be granted to the grieving person to own and express these feelings" (p. 89).

Guilt can also be a troubling emotion to young grievers (Crenshaw, 1990; Wass, 1984b). For example, when a sibling dies after a lengthy illness, surviving brothers or sisters may feel guilty because they resented the special attention the ill child received or felt anger toward their parents who were absorbed with the sibling's needs. Following the death of a classmate, in addition to their sadness, fellow students may feel guilty if they had been "mean" to the deceased or were jealous of extra attention the child received if he or she had been ill for a long time.

POSTTRAUMATIC STRESS DISORDER

When the deaths school-age children experience are violent, grief reactions are usually severe and the likelihood that students will be affected by posttraumatic stress disorders (PTSD) increases. Students (and others) who witness tragic events or who are participants (e.g., in a hostage situation) are especially susceptible. Children and adolescents suffering PTSD have recurring and intrusive memories (e.g., flashbacks or nightmares) and develop generalized feelings of fearfulness and helplessness (Dunne-Maxim, Dunne, & Hauser, 1987; Eth & Pynoos, 1985). Their initial feelings of distress come flooding back, and they reexperience the traumatic event emotionally. Overt symptoms of PTSD include sleep disorders, school phobia, loss of recently acquired skills and knowledge, inability to concentrate, flat affect, irritability, and angry outbursts.

Counselors and teachers who realize that grieving students may develop PTSD can be prepared to take appropriate actions or make referrals. Defusing strong emotions and debriefing students or staff members who are traumatized require special skills that counselors can learn (Janosik, 1986; Petersen & Straub, 1992; Slaikeu, 1990). Some schools, however, prefer to use community mental health professionals who are trained in crisis intervention because school staff may also be traumatized. By addressing the needs of grieving students, instead of ignoring tragic events, school personnel help defuse the psychological distress that causes posttraumatic stress disorders.

Some adults fail to recognize when a child is grieving or suffering PTSD, and others are reluctant to discuss the death because of their own discomfort. Those who do intervene appropriately contribute greatly to the child's psychological well-being. A school counselor (McComb, 1978), commenting on measures taken after the violent death of an elementary teacher in full view of her students, wrote:

> School personnel are to be commended for recognizing how
> psychologically dangerous it would have been for the children

to be allowed to gloss over their unhappy memories. It is essential that children be encouraged to express in a sharing way their
experiences with death . . . . The assumption that silence by the
child means he or she has forgotten the experience is naive.
Such forgetting manifests itself later in unfortunate ways. (p. 95)

STUDENTS WRITE ABOUT LOSS AND GRIEF

Educators can learn much about how loss affects students from their
essays, poems, and letters. Some counselors and teachers who read
students' reflections add their comments before returning them. Students have reported that they find these comments helpful. Most of
the letters, essays, and poems included here were written from 1986
to 1992 by students in the author's loss and grief support groups. Selections have been altered and pseudonyms used to protect the
students' and others' identities.

Usually grief is thought of as emotional pain, but grieving students
frequently refer to somatic feelings or losing a part of themselves physically. One young woman wrote, "When my mother died I lost a very
important part of my life. I lost the inside of me. I mean it felt empty."
After the suicide of a close friend, a student lamented, "When John
died I lost a part of my heart. I didn't know how much of a friend he
was until he was gone. It was like my heart just left." Another wrote,
"When my Grandmother died I lost a great person in my life. She was
always there to talk to me, to feed me, and for anything I needed. When
she died it was like a big chunk had gone out of my stomach."

Death of Friends

Teenagers, more than adults or young children, identify closely with
their peers and spend time and share intimately with them; thus, the
death of a friend can be devastating. Sklar and Hartley (1990, p. 105)
found that adolescents and young adults are a "high risk group for
difficulties that may stem from the death of a close friend" because
friendships at this age are very important. Their research showed that
much support is given in our society to those grieving the death of a
family member, but very little is offered to those grieving a friend's
death. Close friends of the deceased are frequently "disenfranchised
grievers" who suffer from not being accorded the same respect, support,
and sympathy as relatives (Doka, 1989).

**Katrina, who wrote the following letter, felt little support from
her parents when her friend Lisa died.** Katrina was 17 when she entered
her school's loss and grief support group shortly after this death.

Dear Lisa:

I've had a really rough time dealing with your death. In a way, I feel guilty that through your last months I just took them for granted. . . . I love you, Lisa, but feel that [we have] . . . "unfinished business." I want you back so that I could stay involved in your life! I am so sorry I didn't visit you more at the hospital. I wish we could have been closer. . . . I need time to deal with losing you. My parents don't understand that; they think I'm dragging it out and that really hurts.

Katrina's parents could not understand the depth of her grief over the death of a peer. *Unfinished business*, which Katrina mentioned, often complicates the grieving process. The group leader or counselor can help students bring closure to their unfinished business by encouraging them to talk about their regrets or to write a letter to the person who died. Gestalt techniques, especially, are helpful in resolving unfinished business following a death (Alexander & Harman, 1988; Love, 1991, pp. 180–182; Tatelbaum, 1980, chapter 12).

Chee-yun, a 16-year-old, wrote this letter to her boyfriend who was killed in an automobile accident.

I still miss you even though it has been a year. Sometimes I relive the accident. It goes over and over again in my head. When you died I felt as if something that belonged to me and only me had been taken away. I was mad at first. I was mad at you for leaving and at God for taking you. Some of that has gone away, but I still feel so empty. My life is not the same. I look at guys and compare them to you. They never seem to measure up to you. I want to apologize to you for the last fight we had. I know I shouldn't have made such a big deal out of it. I wish I had said that I loved you more often and had let you know how much I cared for you. You stayed with me through thick and thin. You took me with my faults and looked past them. I miss and love you very much.

After a year, Chee-yun still has an emotional attachment to a relationship that ended with her boyfriend's death. Her letter highlights the fact that grief recovery takes time and requires "the adoption of a present and future orientation as hopes, dreams, plans, and aspirations are restructured" (Crenshaw, 1990, p. 24).

Carrie was a 16-year-old whose friend was killed in a hit-and-run accident. While in a loss and grief support group, she wrote the following reaction to the statement "When _____ died I lost _____ ."

When my best friend died, I lost someone very special, someone I loved like a sister, and I still feel like it was my fault that I couldn't be there to help her when the car came zooming by. I feel very lost and lonely. And at times I get so sad still that I don't want to talk or anything. I know I can never have another friend like her. The friends I have now are really nice, but they will never be like Mary.

The group leader wrote the following comments on Carrie's paper before returning it:

You are in pain because you feel guilty for not having been able to prevent the accident. You could not have prevented the accident from happening. You miss your friend because she was like a sister. You miss the close relationship you had. It takes time to heal the hurt. Be patient in experiencing your pain.

Responding to the same statement after a friend's suicide, another group member wrote: "When John died I lost a very close friend with whom I could discuss my problems and . . . [who] was a good listener and always shared my joy and sorrow. He had a way of making me feel better when I was down." **The group leader added these comments:**

You are in pain because of John's death. He was a very close friend who listened to you and shared the good and the bad with you. If you were feeling low, he always tried to cheer you up. You miss this close relationship. Experience your pain. It takes time for the hurt to heal.

Sibling Deaths

Jewett (1982) noted that "in about half of families that suffer the loss of a child, one or more remaining siblings will develop symptoms such as depression, severe separation anxiety, and problems with going to school" (p. 94). The intense rivalries common between siblings may leave a special burden of guilt for surviving brothers and sisters that affects them for years after the death (Crenshaw, 1990). Wass (1984b, p. 120) wrote that "guilt and remorse also arise from memories of fights, teasing, and other negative interactions" with the sibling who died. Siblings may be rivals, but they also have a very strong bond and are frequently dependent on each other for companionship and affection as exemplified in Yolanda's letter, which follows.

Yolanda, a 16-year-old, wrote to her brother who had been murdered the year before at age 20.

> Your death was very tragic for us. Who killed you? Was your death painful? I would just like to say I love you! I always have even if I didn't show it. I would like to apologize for being mean to you. . . . I really liked your determination. Through all your bad times, you hung in there. What a shame that when you were just getting your life together you died. I feel I lost half of me when you died . . . . You were a buddy, a real close friend. I hope justice will be done for what has happened to you.

Marie, a 15-year-old, wrote this letter to her brother who had killed himself 2 years previously.

> I can't believe you are gone. All I can remember is seeing you in the hospital. It was so hard for me to touch or even look at you. I hurt all over. One of the biggest questions I've got for you is why you did it? You knew I loved you and so did Mom and Dad. Maybe I should have told you more often that I loved you. I feel it is my fault. Do you ever think our relationship could've been better? I do. . . . I mean it was pretty good, but I would have liked it to be better. Bill, I'm so sorry for never telling you I loved you. I'm glad that I have your looks, that way I always have something to remember you by. I miss you a lot. I miss talking to you about my problems! When you died I felt I could never trust anyone ever again! I'm afraid that if I get close, I'll lose them. Life is very different without you!

In addition to sadness and loss of trust, Marie, like Yolanda, expressed regret and guilt. Feeling guilt and loss of trust are common themes with children and adolescents who experience the death of someone close (Crenshaw, 1990; Jewett, 1982; Kolehmainen & Handwerk, 1986).

Josh, a 15-year-old, joined the loss and grief group because he **was grieving the death of a baby brother who had been still-born.** He wrote the following letter in the fourth group session.

> Your death was very unexpected. If you had been born one or two days before, you might be here today learning how to sit up. Your death was caused from the umbilical cord being wrapped around your neck several times. . . . When you died, I lost a little brother that I could play with. I could have been someone you looked up to. I'll never have the chance to help you make your first step. I'm trying to cope with your death, and so far I just might have made my first step, something you

would be doing in a few months if you were here. The first step tends to be the hardest.

When a child dies in infancy, there are few, if any, real memories. It is important, however, to acknowledge the life and death and to grieve the "loss of a dream"—what one would have had if the child had lived (Schaefer & Lyons, 1988; Smith & Borgers, 1988–89).

Parent Deaths

Parent deaths are difficult for children of all ages. Depending on their age and developmental stage when the death occurs, some children experience special problems. Furman (1984) pointed out that "children between the ages of 4 to 7 years normally form their own conscience by internalizing their parents' rules and values," and if a parent dies, "this process tends to take place prematurely and the conscience may become excessively harsh and threatening" (p. 201). Adolescents who engage in power struggles with parents feel guilty especially if the parent against whom they rebelled dies. On the other hand, when young children or adolescents idealize the parent, they have difficulty forming new relationships and completing the grief recovery process (Crenshaw, 1990).

Rebecca was 10 when her father died 5 years ago. Her letter reveals that the place he filled in her life is still empty.

> I remember you in the hospital saying "I'll be all right; don't worry about me." I knew you weren't all right, your color was changing. Why didn't you tell me you were dying? I wish that I would have said, "I love you" more often!! I know I said it before you died, but I wish I had said it more often. [When you died] . . . no one paid any attention to me. They thought that Mom took your death harder, but I'm the one who did. My life is not complete without you.
>
> Dad, I really appreciate the times that you were there for me when me and Mom got into fights. . . . Since you died I've felt that nobody cares for me. I wish you could come back . . . . I'll never forget you, Dad.

Because Rebecca has idealized her relationship with her father, she will have difficulty forming new relationships and her grief recovery will be difficult.

Susan's mother died when she was 8 years old. When she came into the loss and grief support group at age 15, Susan was still experiencing emotional pain. She wrote this letter to her deceased mother.

> Well, it has been 7 years since I last saw you. During those 7 years I've been feeling nothing but sadness and grief. I still re-

member clearly when they first told me you were gone. I didn't understand until they told me you were never coming back. At the funeral when they were putting you in the hole in the ground, I wanted to open up the box and take you away.

Our first Christmas without you was so sad, but the best part was when I got the doll house you had bought me. It meant so much to me. And I never forget you on your birthday. But how could I since we have the same birthday. . . . There are so many important events in my life now and I wish you could share them. I'll be 16 soon and I just want you to know that even though you won't be there, you'll always be with me in my heart.

Elizabeth was another 15-year-old whose mother died when she was 8 years old. She had never fully grieved and was in emotional pain. Susan and Elizabeth, by coincidence, were in the same loss and grief group. She wrote:

Mom, why did you have to die? When I told you to stop smoking, why didn't you? You were someone I really cared for. . . . Now Dad is remarried and I don't really like my new mother. She gets mad whenever I try to talk to her. I can't talk to her or Dad. . . . I still have all the clothes you made for me, and I will never throw them away. They're the only memory I have of you. I'm really sorry for not going to your funeral. I really didn't want to because I still couldn't realize what was happening. And, now I finally realize what happened, and I wish I could have gone with you.

This young woman performs well academically, but has a flat affect and cries easily. She has been depressed for several years. As Zinner (1990) observed, "Grief work has few shortcuts and is longer than most expect or our culture allows" (p. 80). Because Susan had never visited her mother's grave, the counselor encouraged her to do so with a close friend or relative.

Roberto, a 17-year-old football player, joined the support group 2 weeks after his father died. Although his parents were divorced and he lived with his mother, Roberto's father had been very important to him. He expressed many regrets about their prior relationship.

Dad, I remember all the good times we used to spend together. I want to know why you had to die suddenly without any warning. I wish I had spent more time finding out about you. I didn't really know anything about your childhood. I regret not talking to you that time I saw you in the mall. When you left me, it felt like everything I had to live for went with you. I know now that I can never make you proud of me, so life really doesn't have any purpose. I just don't care about anything anymore. I wish you could come back, but that's not possible.

After participating in his school's loss and grief group, **Rodney Tyrone Sanders, a 17-year-old, wrote the following poem as a tribute to his mother** who had died 9 months before. His father had been murdered when Rodney was very young. This poem is reprinted with his permission.

Mother

When I was little you were my mother.
But as I grew you became my friend.
When I felt like I couldn't talk to my mother,
I could always talk to my friend.
When you were my friend, you were my best friend.
There was nothing that I didn't feel like
I couldn't talk to you about.
Because when I was feeling down
you were there to turn things around.

Mother, you filled my life with wonderful memories.
You taught me how to be strong when the cards were down.
You gave me hope when I was in despair.
When I felt like I didn't have a friend, I knew that you
would always be there.
Even though I can't see you, I know that you are there
through the love and memories that we once shared.

The love that I used to share with you is still there.
When people see me, they also see you as well.
They see you through the things that you taught me.
You made me the person I am today and I thank you for
raising me the way you did.

I used to wonder what my father was like.
I hate that his life was taken before I could get
to know him.
But you filled both shoes.
There are some parents who have problems
fulfilling just one, but not you.

Mother, I'm sorry that I tried to forget you.
I just felt that the absence of your presence
was too much to bear.
But now I know that the memories of you

will always be there.
The memories are in my heart,
and I'll cherish them always.
The memories you left to me should never be forgotten,
and they never will.

MOTHER, I LOVE YOU!
I WILL NEVER FORGET YOU. I PROMISE.

> —*Rodney T. Sanders*
> *San Antonio, Texas*
> *November, 1991*

Rodney, now an orphan, since both parents have died, writes in the poem of his mother's many sterling qualities and expresses only positive feelings about her. A year after her death, this young man reported that he was still very lonely and depressed. He had much unresolved grief. As Crenshaw (1990) noted, many who grieve express positive feelings easily but "have a hard time recognizing and expressing the negative feelings . . . [and] denied hostile feelings will block their attempts to resolve their grief" (p. 24).

Grandparent Deaths

The death of a grandparent is often a child's first personal experience with death (Glass, 1991) and, along with the death of family pets, the most frequent type of death children experience. Crenshaw (1990, p. 91) noted that "if children are supported in their grieving for the grandparent they will be far better equipped to face the inevitable deaths and losses that come" in the future. Grandparent deaths can be especially difficult even when it is not a first death experience for the child. A special relationship often exists between a grandparent and grandchild, yet the child's mother or father (who is grieving the death of a parent) may fail to recognize how deeply the child is affected. Crenshaw observed that "the loss may be especially acute where the grandparent has lived with the family or been a primary caretaker" (p. 54). Some grandchildren feel guilty about imagined or real "wrongs" they committed against the grandparent, and guilt complicates the grief process. Older children often think that they must be strong for their mother or father who is grieving the loss of a parent.

Kenyon, a 15-year-old, wrote to his grandfather who had been dead for about 2 years.

> I never saw you die. It must have been hard on Grandma. I wish
> I could have been there to say good-bye. But I wasn't and I'm

> sorry. I'm also sorry for not writing you. I guess I was just lazy. You were good to me. When you died I didn't cry. I had to be strong for Mom. But I do miss you very much.

Kenyon expressed regrets for not writing and guilt over his failure to cry. As is typical, he believed that he needed to be strong for his grieving mother.

Laurie was 15 when her grandfather died. She wrote this letter about the special part he played in her life. As Laurie mentions, holidays are especially hard following the death of a beloved family member.

> I've missed you so, so much! My life seems so lonely without you. You always made me smile. You brought joy to our whole family, but especially me. The holidays are the worst days of all because we know you will not be there to brighten the day. You gave me so much courage to do things I didn't think I could do. I loved doing those crossword puzzles with you until early in the morning. When I do them now, I want to cry because that was our favorite thing to do together. There isn't one day I don't think about you.

Angela, a 16-year-old, was upset that she did not see her grandfather before he died and had regrets over her prior behavior.

> Grandpa, I really wish I had had a chance to say goodbye. Mom [and the others] got to see you in the hospital. I wish I could've gone to cheer you up, or just to talk to you. I really loved you a lot, and hope that you know that, although I may not have said it enough. I'm sorry that sometimes I acted very selfish and immature . . . [and] made our visits unpleasant. I always loved when you'd come stay at our house. I loved having you around to joke with and you were always happy. When you died, I felt a huge loss. I felt not only the loss of my grandfather, but also the loss of a great friend.

The special relationship that often exists between grandparent and grandchild is evident in this letter. As an important step toward resolving her grief, Angela identifies specifically what she lost when her grandfather died—someone to joke with her, to cheer her up, a great friend.

After her parents divorced, **Stephanie lived with her grandmother and grandfather for 3 years until they died** (both within a 12-month period). In a letter written a few weeks after her grandfather's death, this teenager recalled their special relationship.

Grandpa: You were like my best friend . . . . I probably told you everything, well almost everything. I knew that if I told you anything you wouldn't tell a soul! You meant so much to me. I never wanted you to die. I wish I had told you how much I loved you more often. I miss you so much. I don't have anyone to stick up for me like you did. With you and grandma gone, it's like I'm on my own now. If you were still here I would be going to church and I'd be having a lot more fun. My dad is real strict and I miss you so much and just wish you were still here with me. I wish that one wish would come true!

Stephanie, like Angela, identifies what she lost when this special person died—a confidant, a protector, someone to take her to church. Grief therapist Judy Tatelbaum (1980) stressed that resolving grief "hinges on our admitting *what* we lost. Knowing precisely what is now gone enables us to grieve fully . . ." (p. 111).

A young girl, Twyla, wrote to her grandmother who had been ill for several years.

I don't understand why you got this disease. How did you get cancer? Why did you get so skinny? It was weird when you died. It was like a part of me was torn away. Before you died, I wanted to tell you how much you meant to me and that I loved you. I wanted to tell you that I believed you could make it. You could live a few more years. I wanted to drill that into your head. We were pretty close, but we didn't talk that much. I wish we had.

This was Twyla's first experience with death and she was left with many questions and regrets. She had tried to "will" her grandmother back to good health, reminiscent of young children's use of *magical thinking*, a concept discussed earlier in this chapter.

SUMMARY

Counselors and teachers who want to understand how grief affects their students have many learning opportunities. They can observe their students, listen to them, and read what they write about their grief. They can enroll in college courses or workshops offered locally or attend sessions on grief counseling at professional conferences. Although formal educational opportunities may be limited, other resources—books, journal articles, and films—are readily available to those who want to become knowledgeable, effective helpers.

CHAPTER 4

Facilitating Healthy Grief Responses

Dying used to be openly discussed in our society, but sex was obscene. Now sex is openly discussed and dying is obscene. (Dr. David Belgum, in Powers, 1971)

As the medical doctor and professor of religion Dr. David Belgum (Powers, 1971, p. 76) observed 20 years ago, death has replaced sex as the forbidden topic in our death- and grief-denying society. Public attitudes do not seem to have changed over the past two decades and may account for the "paucity of death education in the schools" (Wass, Miller, & Thornton, 1990, p. 261). A recent study conducted in both rural and urban areas of Florida found that 80% of the students in grades 5 through 12 "never" or "seldom" talked to their parents about death (Wass et al., 1989). Few public schools offer regular opportunities for students to discuss death and dying. Wass et al. (1990) found that only 11% of U.S. public schools offered a course or unit on death education and only 17% had grief support programs. Of the schools studied, 25% did have suicide prevention/intervention programs. However, most of the grief support and suicide programs were crisis-oriented, not developmental. In a recent commentary on the need for developmental death education and grief support programs in schools, two medical school professors wrote:

> Death is a topic most teachers would rather not discuss, let alone teach. It is easy to understand why surveys show that very few elementary-school teachers deal with the subject in any planned manner in their classes. Death is an uncomfortable topic. . . . [Yet] virtually all children, by the time they reach school age, have had some experience with death that is significant to them. Avoiding the subject in school and at home only creates more mystery and fear. (Schonfeld & Kappelman, 1992, p. 25)

The reluctance to discuss death is unfortunate because the prevalence of death in the lives of school-age children is increasing. An extensive study conducted in 1980 showed that the major crises in students' lives are the death of a parent, sibling, or friend and their parents' divorce or separation (Allan & Anderson, 1986). A more recent study (Glass, 1991) of middle school students in North Carolina showed that "41% of the students had been personally involved with death within the past year" and over half had experienced other types of loss. Other statistics indicate that parents of between 7,000 and 12,000 children in the United States commit suicide annually (Dunne-Maxim, Dunne, & Hauser, 1987). If current trends continue, one of every six children who are 18 and younger will have at least one of their parents die (Van Dexter, 1986). If one adds to the deaths of parents and relatives the increasing number of violent deaths of school-age children, it seems unlikely that *any* school-age child will reach adulthood without experiencing a loss related to death.

With so many students affected by loss and grief each year, in a death- and grief-denying society, can there be any question about the important role schools have to play? Grief therapist Alan Wolfelt (1983) stressed that "education with children should begin before, not after, a death experience. More specifically, death education should occur throughout children's development whenever an appropriate 'teachable' moment arises" (p. 6). Teachers and counselors are essential to the success of programs designed to teach about death or to assist those who are grieving.

ACQUIRING HELPING SKILLS

Many grief therapists (Crenshaw, 1990; Wolfelt, 1983; Zinner, 1987) have reported that early intervention with "survivors" (i.e., the friends, relatives, and others who were close to the deceased) is vital to ensure healthy grieving. Unfortunately, as James and Cherry (1988) observed, "We are better prepared to deal with minor accidents than we are to deal with the grief caused by death. Simple first aid gets more attention in our world than death and emotional loss" (p. 12). Because school counselors and teachers provide the first line of defense in assisting grieving students, those who are not prepared to respond to grief reactions should be trained before a crisis occurs. Potential helpers can acquire the knowledge and skills needed for early intervention by attending special workshops or reading books and articles on the subject. Many publications (see Appendix A) are available for those who want to learn about the grieving process, how to talk to children about death, and helping strategies.

Although adults who teach or counsel grieving students do not need extensive training, they should be comfortable with the topic of death and grief reactions and know appropriate helping strategies

(Jewett, 1982; Jones, 1977). Corr (1984) wrote that being helpful is within the capability of most interested adults:

> In general, they will need an opportunity and some direction for examining their own perceptions of death, a certain amount of information, an appreciation of typical concerns of children, a chance to benefit from the viewpoints of others, and practice in elementary interactions skills. (p. 49)

Workshops are available for professionals who need training to help grieving students and for parents who wish to understand how loss affect children (Knowles & Reeves, 1983; Wolfelt, 1983, chapters 4 & 5). *The Grief Recovery Handbook: A Step-by-Step Program for Moving Beyond Loss* (James & Cherry, 1988) provides information and exercises for adults who need to recover from their own losses before offering to help others.

EDUCATING STUDENTS ABOUT GRIEF

Counselors and teachers can assist grieving students by listening, allowing them to experience their feelings, and not expecting them to resolve their grief too quickly. However, it is also important to give students accurate information about death and the grieving process. Education can "help students dispel myths and confront the anxieties and uncertainties surrounding loss, death, and grief. . . [and] be better prepared to cope with these experiences" (Glass, 1991, pp. 144–145).

Oates (1988) suggested that there are specific messages young grievers need to hear:

1. Emotional pain, like physical pain, has a beginning, a middle, and an end. Physical wounds do not heal without time and attention—the same is true of emotional wounds.
2. Responses to loss are varied and do not necessarily manifest the degree of grief one feels. Some people shed tears readily, others do not. The only "bad" grief is that which is unexpressed.
3. Our bad thoughts or words do not cause others to die. Likewise, our "if only's"—"If only I had told someone about her talk of suicide"—could not have prevented the death.
4. Feeling anger at the person who died or at God or the world in general is normal when grieving. . . . Accepting and acknowledging . . . feelings rather than avoiding them helps relieve the pain of the grief experience.

5. Most grieving individuals go through several well-defined stages of grief before they find relief from their emotional pain. Young grievers need to be taught these stages and facilitated in their progress through them.
6. Recovery is not a straight shot, but rather takes place in an upward, but jagged pattern. There will be good days and bad. (p. 90)

Colgrove, Bloomfield, and McWilliams (1976) provided other messages that may be helpful. For example: "If you find photographs and mementos helpful to the mourning process, use them" (p. 62); and "Now is not the time to alter your eating habits drastically or go on a crash diet. Good nutrition tends to speed the healing process" (p. 68). Young grievers are inexperienced and need to know in concrete terms how to take care of themselves in an emotional crisis.

Activities to facilitate healthy grieving may be developmental, that is, used before a death occurs, or responsive—used after a death. How activities and strategies are implemented depends on the expertise and comfort level of the teacher or counselor, the grade level of the students, and the circumstances of the death. Helpers must also be aware of how sociocultural backgrounds and settings affect students' concepts of death and expressions of grief (Kalish & Reynolds, 1981). The activities described below have been used in group and individual counseling and in classrooms by the author and others who counsel students or teach about death and dying. Readers who want detailed information about these activities can consult the articles and books cited.

CLASSROOM GUIDANCE UNITS

Classroom guidance units that are well planned, focused in content, and taught over a period of weeks or months are useful in preparing students to cope with life's crises. Effective units not only give information, but also help students develop coping strategies and identify resources they can use when a crisis occurs. Unfortunately, a recent study (Wass et al., 1990) found that "classroom-based death education is offered in less than a fifth of the middle and high schools, and seldom at the elementary level" (p. 261). Although a few efforts at establishing death education programs were made in the mid-1970s, these failed to gain wide acceptance. Today, the number of programs in public schools is similar to that of a decade ago.

Mueller (1978) described one of these early attempts, a 3-day unit for fifth graders that infused topics on death and dying into the subject areas of spelling, math, social studies, health, music, and English. He believed that the unit, which used a variety of activities including a visit to a funeral home, was beneficial to his students. His method was criticized, however, as a "shotgun approach to the subject" by an elementary teacher and mother of seven (Freeman, 1978). She was especially concerned with the 3-day time span:

> A number of Mueller's class activities would be valuable . . . if not crowded into such an intensive study period. Over a longer time span—a semester or even a school year—students could probably gain valuable insights . . . from the filmstrip viewings and discussions, the song analysis, the creative writing assignments, the role playing. (p. 118)

Allan and Anderson (1986) developed a six-phase classroom guidance unit on childhood crises with several 40-minute lessons. Counselors taught these lessons to students in grades 2, 5, and 8, while the students' teachers observed. Activities included having students brainstorm the "biggest crises that happen to children," discuss these events, write essays and draw pictures related to a crisis, and finally, consider ways of coping in times of crisis. The counselors and teachers were surprised at "the number of death experiences children reported and how readily children talked about them . . . [and that] although the event may have been some years passed, children were still aware of the feelings they experienced" (p. 146).

One important phase of this unit helped students identify their own strengths and learn coping strategies. At first, the students had difficulty believing that anything would help. However, as they shared experiences, the students identified many coping strategies: talking with teachers, counselors, or friends; crying; writing in journals; talking to pets; using problem-solving strategies; getting a second opinion; praying; and relaxing. In evaluating the unit, the authors noted that "although there was considerable disclosure of painful experiences, there was little evidence that the children felt overwhelmed" (p. 144).

As the program above illustrates, successful units can be presented using materials readily available in any classroom; however, some teachers use selected videos (see Appendix A) to enhance their instruction. *Dying is Part of Living* is appropriate for use in health, home economics, and social studies classes with students in grades 7 through 12 as part of a unit on coping with life crises. *As We Learn to Fall: A Look at Death and Grief and Coping and Living* can be used in grades 4 to 12, and *Blackberries in the Dark*, based on the novel by Mavis Jukes (1985), is suggested for grades 4 to 6 to help students explore their own feelings about death and dying. Teachers should preview videos carefully and choose those that relate to their learning objectives.

Many different activities can be included in units that teach about loss and grief. For example, students can complete The Loss Inventory for Kids found in *Helping Children Cope With Grief* (Wolfelt, 1983) and modeled after a life stress scale developed for adults (Holmes & Rahe, 1967). This inventory addresses the cumulative effects of loss events that occur within a specific time period. The Death Anxiety Scale or other death attitude scales (Lonetto & Templer, 1986) may be useful as pre- and postevaluation measures. Inventory results give students insight into their fears and attitudes and foster discussions about how to cope with loss both now and in the future. The loss graph or time-line discussed later in this chapter is another activity appropriate for use in a classroom unit.

Classroom units that teach about loss, death, and grief can be developed using literature appropriate for students' ages, reading levels, and interests. Several resources (viz., Adler, Stanford, & Adler, 1976; Bernstein, 1989; Wass & Corr, 1984b) give examples or descriptions of useful materials. Teachers and counselors should be selective, however, in choosing literature. One study (Moore & Mae, 1987) found that many children's books do not portray the grief process accurately. Wolfelt (1983) suggested that teachers or counselors ask these questions before choosing a book to teach about loss:

> What message would the child get from the book? How are feelings dealt with in the book? Are the content and language in the book appropriate for the developmental level of the child? How does the book define death? How could the book best be used with children? Does the book represent a general humanistic approach to death or a particular religious point of view? (p. 154)

Several authors (Bernstein, 1989; Griggs, 1977; Wolfelt, 1983) described literature related to loss and recommended guidelines for its use. Wass and Corr (1984b) compiled an annotated resource guide of materials (print and other media) that teachers can use in teaching about death. Stanford (1977b) discussed infusing death education into the established school curriculum, suggested topics and resources, and provided teaching guides for social studies, language arts, science, health, and home economics classes. Gordon and Klass (1979) outlined a program of death education with suggested curricula and specific resources and activities for grade levels K-12.

OTHER ACTIVITIES

Because not all grieving students discuss their thoughts and feelings spontaneously or in response to questioning, counselors and teachers need a variety of helping strategies. Activities and strategies to facilitate healthy grieving are unlimited and may include written expressions, creative arts (Gladding, 1992), or memorial tributes.

Writing Activities

When a young, popular high school math teacher (who also directed the pep squad and dance team) died unexpectedly in her sleep, there was considerable schoolwide trauma (Oates, 1988). The day the death was announced, the math department chairperson and a school psychologist met with the deceased teacher's classes. The psychologist encouraged students to express their feelings verbally and to write essays or letters to provide "an avenue for catharsis and closure" (p. 95). Often when a teacher dies, students feel guilty over past thoughts or deeds, and these feelings need to be expressed. One student wrote in his letter, "Thank you for helping me and for being my friend. I'm sorry if I did anything to offend you in any way, that's the last thing I ever wanted to do. I wish I could see you . . . just to say 'good-bye.' " Another student wrote, "Miss Brown will always be special to me, even though I did get mad at her sometimes. I just wish I had a little more time to tell her how sorry I am . . . and that I really loved her." Another penned these thoughts, "It's so sad because she was just there and happy and talking about her wedding . . . . She was so young, and her whole life was ahead of her. It's so scary to see that she died that young." In their essays and letters, many students expressed regret about things they had done or said and wrote that it was frightening that their teacher died so young. The death of a young teacher, much like the death of a peer, shatters students' illusions of invulnerability and immortality. When they realize that death does happen to people they know and to those near their own age, suddenly the world seems less safe.

To help students express their thoughts and feelings following a violent death, one elementary counselor placed a large glass jar in the classroom (Collison et al., 1987). The father of one of the students had been murdered at a nearby junior high school where he was principal, and the incident had received much publicity. Students in the classroom wrote a comment, question, or concern on a piece of paper and placed it in the jar. Each day the counselor drew several papers from the container and talked with students. This procedure was still being used a year and a half after the tragedy. After a tragic death, teachers or counselors may ask students to write news stories about the event to read in a mock television newscast, prepare questions to ask a police officer, ambulance driver, or eyewitness, or write a script for a trial. Having students dramatize or role play these written activities can facilitate healthy resolution of disturbing thoughts and feelings.

Older children and teenagers may find comfort in keeping a journal of their thoughts and feelings in the days following the death. A teacher or counselor can explain this technique, noting that it should not become a chore—students do not need to write in the journal every day. If the student shares his or her journal with a teacher or counselor, the adult must respect the privacy of the information. If grieving students cannot write because they are too young or have handicaps, their thoughts and feelings can be recorded on audio- or videotapes.

Artwork

Art activities can be helpful when working with children who have difficulty verbalizing their feelings. Students can make drawings or paintings, clay structures, collages, and papier-maché creations. Finger paints are especially useful in expressing feelings. *The Art of Grief* (Raymer & McIntyre, 1987) provides examples and explanations of how to use art as therapy with children and how to interpret symbols or pictures children draw. Grief therapist David Crenshaw (1990), who uses artwork frequently in his work with bereaved children, wrote, "Once it is down on paper it is easier to get children to talk about the details of the experience, which often brings into focus the feelings that have been so hard for them to express" (p. 85).

Students can draw pictures of an activity they enjoyed doing with the deceased. They can use photographs or cut pictures from magazines to make a collage showing the deceased person (alone or with the student) engaged in favorite activities. Students can make a coat of arms, poster, or classroom mural about the student or teacher who died to depict activities that remind them of the deceased or to show what this person meant to them. Although preparing artwork may seem trivial, such activities evoke strong feelings in some students. *Time should always be allowed for processing the feelings that surface.*

Memorial Tributes

Often when a tragic death occurs, survivors feel powerless, therefore doing something tangible or taking some action seems to help. When the young teacher who had been the pep squad sponsor died, the school counselor brought art supplies and writing paper to the pep squad class and had students prepare drawings, essays, and poems on several topics (e.g., *"A Flower That Reminds Me of Miss Brown," "A Typical Pep*

Squad Practice Session," and *"My Favorite Memory"*). Each student shared her creation with a group of 12 others; then each group chose one essay and one drawing to be presented to the class of 150 students. Oates (1988) reported that "some of the creations were sad and some were funny. They were all quite moving; corporate sharing seems to facilitate healthy grieving. The girls decided to have the essays and drawings placed in a notebook as a memorial tribute to be given to Miss Brown's parents" (p. 95). Several teachers at the school prepared the notebook with headings and colorful dividers before it was given to the parents.

Several months after six teenagers from one high school in Sandwich, Illinois, died in an automobile accident, a grief counselor encouraged survivors to share the poetry and music that had helped them deal with their grief (Schaefer & Lyons, 1988). Students and family friends prepared "a booklet called 'Thanks for the Memories,' a collection of poems, stories, and sketches about the dead girls, done by their friends and families . . . the reminiscences of a community that mourned, then pulled out of grief" (p. 56).

Students can collect money for an organization that supports medical research or a program that held a special interest for the deceased (e.g., the local animal shelter or a food bank). Depending on the type of death, a more lasting tribute may be appropriate. Placing the picture of a deceased teacher in a special place in the school, planting a memorial tree or flower garden, establishing a scholarship fund in the name of the deceased, or placing a special book in the library are often used as tributes.

Some crisis specialists believe that memorials following a suicide should be minimized to avoid glamorizing the event (Barrett, 1989; CDC, August 19, 1988; Phi Delta Kappa, 1988). Siehl (1990), however, argued that memorial services or other special events after a suicide death "help students draw closure to the death and tragedy and help them to begin to go on with their work and lives" (p. 55). Instead of planning a memorial to the student who took his or her life, students' energies can be directed toward helping the living. They can volunteer to answer crisis telephone hotlines, become tutors for younger children, or serve as peer helpers on their own campus.

COUNSELING TECHNIQUES AND STRATEGIES

Some activities used in classroom guidance units are also effective in group or individual counseling. Many different techniques and strategies are available to those who counsel with grieving students. The counselor's theoretical orientation, age of the counselees, and the time available for counseling will determine those selected. Some helpful techniques and strategies are described in this section, and others are detailed in the group counseling outlines in chapter 5.

Therapeutic Play

Crenshaw (1990) recommended play therapy for bereaved children, noting that it provides the "psychological distance they need to work out their feelings" (p. 83). Schaefer and Lyons (1988) wrote that play helps a child "achieve mastery over a situation he doesn't understand and work through his anxiety. Some children paint sad pictures, others might play violent games in which cars crash and burn to let their feeling out" (p. 92). Counselors and teachers may choose from many types of therapeutic play.

Modeling clay or play dough is one medium that young children seem to enjoy. Child psychologist Dr. Violet Oaklander (1988) suggested that the "tactile and kinesthetic experience" found in working with clay provides a "good link to verbal expression for nonverbal children" (p. 67). Grieving children are often angry, but may not recognize or be able to verbalize this emotion. Working with clay gives children an avenue for venting anger by building things and smashing them. Modeling clay can also be used to make replicas of an object that reminds students of the person who died or to craft gifts for others who are grieving.

Puppetry has been used in death education (Bernardt & Praeger, 1985), group guidance (Egge, Marks, & McEvers, 1987), and counseling (Oaklander, 1988) to help children express feelings and handle conflict. Carter (1987) described in detail the use of puppets with a 10-year-old fifth grader named Steven, who developed severe behavior and learning problems after witnessing his father's murder. Because he strongly resisted verbal counseling and refused to talk about his father (saying that "talking about his father made him mad"), Steven's counselor chose nondirective play therapy. The counselor reported that during their third session Steven showed little sadness or other emotion as he played.

> With no instructions, prompting, . . . or approval from the counselor, Steven began to play with the puppet family . . . [smashing] the two men and the mother figure together with frenetic violence . . . . Eventually the father puppet was shot. Steven staged the funeral, complete with the church sermon, the procession to the graveyard, and the lowering of the casket into the ground. (p. 211)

In subsequent sessions, Steven's puppets displayed much violence, anger, and aggression, but no sadness. In session 8, however, when the father puppet fell off a high wire while performing in a circus, "Steven cried, 'My daddy died . . . oh no, my daddy died. Don't let him die. What am I going to do? My daddy died' " (p. 212). After this emotional incident, Steven shared his thoughts and feelings about his father's death openly and verbally.

Sand is another effective medium for play therapy with bereaved children. Vinturella and James (1987) described in detail six counseling sessions with Chris,* an 8-year-old boy who became overly aggressive at school, but distant from his mother after his father died. When he entered the play therapy room, which had a variety of media, Chris went immediately to the sand table. Speculating on why this child chose the sand table over other objects, the authors wrote, "Perhaps Chris discovered a medium that he could control and shape, something he could not do with the death of his father or with his own feelings surrounding that death" (p. 229).

In the first session, Chris used the sand and toy figures to recreate the scene of his father's grave site, but placed his father on top of the grave. He put up a brave front and told the story of his father's death and funeral unemotionally. In subsequent sessions Chris returned to his original sand picture, but rearranged the characters representing himself, his father, and his mother as he explored his feeling with the counselor. In session 3, Chris finally buried his father beneath the sand. With the counselor's gentle prodding, Chris had begun to express his need to be held by his mother even when he was acting brave, his anger toward his father for leaving him, and, in session 4, "his fear that his mother would also die soon, leaving him totally alone." Chris's mother attended session 5 and reassured him that they would have a long life together. Chris and his mother constructed "a sand picture representing their new life together [and] bonded in a new way as they both told the story of how they would like things to be for them" (p. 237).

Bibliotherapy

Teachers may include literature in curriculum units on death and dying, as discussed in the section titled "Classroom Guidance Units." When literature is used in counseling, it is referred to as *bibliotherapy*. Bernstein (1989) and Gladding and Gladding (1991) described the use of bibliotherapy, including its benefits and limitations, skills needed by the facilitator, and a step-by-step guide for initiating the procedure with individuals or groups of students. When using bibliotherapy, the counselor selects appropriate material and has the student(s) read a portion before each counseling session. The counselor and student(s) discuss both the content of the material and the feelings and ideas

---

*Excerpted by permission from "Sandplay: A Therapeutic Medium With Children," 1987. Elementary School Guidance and Counseling, 21, pp. 229–238.

generated from the reading. According to Gladding and Gladding, bibliotherapy "provides an avenue for the release of pent-up emotions that may have previously prevented constructive personal growth and interpersonal interaction." A book about an athlete's struggle with cancer and subsequent death allows students "to release feelings not only associated with [this] death but with other significant losses they may have experienced and not resolved" (p. 11).

Loss Graph or Time-Line

Counselors have used the loss history graph or time-line successfully with people of all ages—very young children, adolescents, and adults (James & Cherry, 1988; Jewett, 1982). In this technique students discuss the types of losses they have experienced. Older students make a list of their losses in chronological order. (Using this technique with young children is discussed below.) Students draw a horizontal line on a piece of paper with "0" written at one end of the line and their current age at the other. Using the list, each student writes his or her losses on a time-line or graph, drawing a vertical line downward at the age the loss occurred to represent the depth of the loss. For example, if a student's first loss was her dog's death when she was 3, the vertical line may be short, but the line for her boyfriend's death when she was 15 may be quite long. Besides deaths, students frequently include parents' divorce, break-up of a romantic relationship, and moving as loss events. Students share information from the graphs and their feelings about the losses with the counseling group or with the counselor in an individual session.

In her work with young children, Jewett (1982, pp. 100–103) tied a piece of yarn between two chairs and attached photos or drawings representing the "lost" person (or loss event) in chronological order. She used cards showing faces with different expressions to connect feelings with the events. Using the completed time-line as a visual aid, she encouraged the child to tell a story about these losses. When working with children in foster care (leaving one home for another is a significant loss event), Jewett cut houses from colored paper and clipped them to the line to represent the child's many homes. She drew pictures on each house of the family members who lived there. Visual representations and related stories help children make sense of multiple or sequential losses.

Storytelling

Many grief therapists (Crenshaw, 1990; Haasl & Marnocha, 1990; Wolfelt, 1983) use storytelling in their work with children of all ages. Oaklander (1988) wrote about her creative use of this technique:

The use of stories in therapy involves making up my own stories to tell to children; the children's making up stories; reading stories from books; writing stories; dictating stories; using things to stimulate stories such as pictures, projective tests, puppets, the flannel board, the sand tray, drawings, open-ended fantasies; and using props and aids such as tape recorder, video tape, walkie-talkies, toy microphone, or an imaginary TV set. (p. 85)

Some storytelling techniques involve fantasy monologues, and others are interactive, with the grieving child supplying parts of the story. In a fantasy monologue the counselor may tell the child that he or she "knows another child whose sister died" and relate a story about what this other child said, felt, or thought after the death. This technique normalizes grief reactions and often helps grieving children recognize their own sadness or accept their "unacceptable" feelings (e.g., anger or guilt). This technique can be used to test for thoughts and feelings that the counselor believes the child is experiencing, but has not expressed. For example, in working with a boy whose father died, Wolfelt (1983, p. 141) suggested that the counselor have the fictional child say that after *his* dad died, he told his mother he was too sick to come to school when actually he was afraid of leaving her. He was afraid that she might die too. With mutual storytelling, the child writes (or recites) a story with the counselor's help. The counselor begins the story by reading an opening sentence or two, then asks the student to supply the next sentence. Depending on the circumstances of the death, the counselor guides the story content to address anger, guilt, resentment, wishful thinking, and other issues.

Metaphors

Many grief counselors (Crenshaw, 1990; Grollman, 1990; Jewett, 1982; Oaklander, 1988) use therapeutic metaphors in their work with children. Metaphors are useful in helping children (and adults) understand the concept of death and grief. Frequently the metaphors relate death or grief to things in nature. One metaphor, used by the author, compares grief to a snowball:

While playing on the mountain top, you are hit by a small snowball or even several. You feel the pain, but are not overwhelmed. Small snowballs cause little pain and melt quickly. However, if you run from the snowball, and it rolls on the ground behind you, it becomes larger and larger. The snowball is very quiet, but you always know it is there and keep looking back to be sure it isn't getting too close. One day, when you can run no more, the giant snowball hits you with all its force and the pain is immense.

That's how grief is. Although we run from grief or deny it, it is still there. All the time we refuse to acknowledge our grief, it is present and keeps us looking backward instead of forward. And one day the grief overtakes us and the pain seems unbearable. If we encounter our grief fully at the time of the loss, the pain will not overwhelm us.

In another methaphor the author compares a child's feelings following the sudden death of a loved one to the anger, outrage, and helplessness a child experiences when a sandcastle is destroyed.

You have spent the day on the beach constructing the most intricate of all sandcastles. You feel satisfied and safe in the warm sunlight. Suddenly the tide comes up and washes your creation away in an instant (or someone kicks it into many pieces either accidentally or purposefully). Helpless to undo the damage, you feel outraged and angry at the other person or the sea. You tell yourself, "If only I had constructed this farther from the water; if only the other person had not been so careless or so mean; if only . . . ." Your bright spirits and feeling of security are dashed forever, or so it seems. You will never build another sandcastle as long as you live, at least not one that beautiful! That's how grief feels when someone we love dies unexpectedly.

Family Constellation

Making a family constellation (or constellation of friends after a peer's death) to show how members of the family or friendship group related to one another before and how they relate to each other after the death helps grieving students move beyond denial. The counselor gives each student several cardboard circles approximately 2 inches in diameter. Students write the names of family or friends on these (one name per circle), using a different colored pen to write the name of the deceased. Students then manipulate the circles into a configuration showing how their family members or friends related before the death (i.e., who was closest to whom, who supported whom, or who spent time together). In a counseling group or with the counselor in an individual session, each student describes the interactions in his or her family (or group of friends) before the death and shares thoughts and feelings. Students are instructed to remove the deceased person's circle from their constellation and reorder the circles to represent how the family (or friends) relate to one another now. Students share their thoughts and feelings about the "after death" grouping.

Empty Chair

The Gestalt technique referred to as *empty chair* can be used with grieving students. Students imagine that the deceased is sitting in an empty chair or at a desk and speak to the deceased as if he or she were there. Following the suicide of a 13-year-old middle school boy named Jason, a school counselor used this technique with grieving students in class-sized groups, small groups, and individually (Alexander & Harman, 1988). The counselor wanted to help the students say their "good-byes" to Jason, to finish an *unfinished gestalt*. Using the empty chair technique, students spoke to Jason's empty desk, telling him of their feelings (e.g., anger, confusion, guilt, and sadness). Some students told Jason what they might have done if they had known he was troubled. To facilitate closure, the counselor encouraged students to end their remarks with a good-bye statement. Students who chose not to speak were "invited to look at Jason's seat and imagine saying goodbye to him and to imagine telling him what they would like him to know" (p. 284). The counselor who worked with these students had been in Gestalt therapy training for 2 years and recommended that counselors *not* use Gestalt techniques unless they have a good understanding of related theory and appropriate skills.

SUMMARY

The classroom units, activities, strategies, and counseling techniques discussed in this chapter can be helpful to those who teach about loss or assist grieving students. Armed with knowledge, understanding, and compassion, counselors and teachers can provide many opportunities for students to learn about the grief process (preferably, before a death occurs) and help them to share their feelings following a death. Principals must work with teachers and counselors to ensure that these opportunities are available.

CHAPTER 5

Leading Loss and Grief Groups

Children who have a set time to talk about their loss . . . are more likely to be able to focus themselves on school work . . . . A school counselor or psychologist can [provide] a place at school where it is all right to think about the loss, instead of always having to attend to class responsibilities. This helps the child see school as an understanding rather than a hostile environment. (Jewett, 1982)

When a death affects a school campus, students suffer from the initial shock of the news and often need to process their feelings immediately. Teachers or counselors can assist many students in a classroom setting, as described in the case study in chapter 6 about Maria Leal, a student who died in an automobile accident. Other students may be helped by a one-session group experience led by a teacher or counselor who is comfortable responding to grieving students. Most students can return to their daily routine after a brief period of well-facilitated sharing. As one 16-year-old student said, "I'm not looking for answers because I know there aren't any. All I want is someone who will listen. Is that asking too much?" Students who are more deeply affected by a death may profit from participating in a multiple-session support group (Alexander & Harman, 1988; Baxter, 1982; Gray, 1988; Haasl & Marnocha, 1990; Lieberman & Borman, 1979).

Extensive training is not required to be helpful to students (Corr, 1984; Jones, 1977), but counselors and teachers who possess group facilitation skills and have accurate information (e.g., on teenage suicide or the stages of grief recovery) are more effective. Leaders of ongoing support groups will need additional knowledge and skills. Wolfelt (1983) provided information and practice activities to train those who wish to be a "Helping-Healing-Adult" for grieving children. Counselors and teachers can also learn to be effective helpers by co-facilitating groups with other mental health professionals, attending specialized training workshops, and reading about grief recovery.

A single-session group experience (that can be used after a student suicide, other type of student death, or death of a teacher) and an eight-session grief support group are outlined below. The support group is not a psychotherapy group, and students who need in-depth counseling should be referred to other professionals who have the expertise and time to facilitate their recovery. Specialized loss and grief groups are available in many communities. Freeman (1991) described an eight-session community-based psychotherapy group for suicide survivors. Brown (1991) and Redmond (1989) discussed guidelines for group counseling with individuals whose friends or relatives were murdered. Some of the techniques and strategies these writers reported can be adapted for a school-based support group. In schools, groups usually meet once a week for 1 hour (or the length of a class period) for 6 to 12 weeks. The logistics of scheduling groups during the school day are discussed later in this chapter.

GUIDES FOR ONE-SESSION SUPPORT GROUPS

The guides presented in this section have been used with middle and high school students. Many activities and strategies, with minor modifications, are appropriate for counseling younger children.

Student Death by Suicide

This guide assumes that students already know the facts related to their schoolmate's suicide. If they do not, the leader gives factual information to discourage speculation and rumors. If the size of the group is small enough, students should sit in a circle with the leader.

　　1. Have students identify themselves by first name and tell the group how they knew this student. Encourage students to share how they learned about the death, the last time they talked to or saw the student, or one thing they remember about the deceased. Ask questions beginning with a student who is likely to share openly. (If the first student declines to answer, others will often follow this example.) State that it is all right to "pass" on any question.

　　2. If students talk freely, simply reflect their feelings while reinforcing the idea that it is good to experience our feelings. Identifying and experiencing feelings represents healthy versus unhealthy grieving.

　　3. If students do not talk freely, or after their initial sharing, ask the following questions:

- If you could ask *(name of student who died)* one question now, what would it be?
- If you could say one thing to *(name of student)*, what would it be?

- How do you feel right now about this loss?—angry, resentful, frightened, lonely, empty inside, confused?
- Is it natural to think about killing oneself?
- When someone says, "I just wish I were dead," what does the person want?
- What can we do if we believe someone is thinking about suicide?

4. The leader should make these points in the session:

- Almost everyone thinks of suicide at one time or another; it is not unnatural to do so.
- Suicidal thoughts are reactions to emotional pain or despair, but *there is no need to act on these thoughts*. People who feel their thoughts are getting out of control should seek help.
- Emotional pain, like physical pain, does end—it has a *beginning* (characterized by great pain, despair, or embarrassment), a *middle,* and an *end*. Describe the intense pain of a severe burn that gradually gets better and eventually heals. (Young people do not have the life experience to know that emotional pain, like physical pain, will end.)
- The normal response to a death, particularly by suicide, includes: *Shock and disbelief*—"This can't be true." "I feel like it is just a bad dream." *Anger or resentment*—"Why did she have to do this?" "Didn't she know how much she had to live for, or how much we would hurt . . .? Didn't she care about us?" *Guilt*—"I shouldn't be angry with someone who's dead." "What did I do (or not do) that caused this?" "If she had a problem, she would have told me. We told each other everything." "If I had only . . ."
- *A suicide attempt* or statement about wanting to die *is always a cry for help*, an attempt to communicate that "My life is unbearable; please do something to help me (or find someone to help me) out of this situation." What people want when they are hurting emotionally is not to get out of this world, but to get out of the present situation—to end the bad feelings.
- There is no one answer to "why" someone commits suicide; the answers are as varied as the individuals who choose to end their lives. Instead of dwelling on the "why," we can use our time better by learning to recognize when someone is suicidal and doing what we can to see that the person gets help.

- Feeling low or sad or blue is a normal reaction to life, as normal as feeling happy and hopeful. Bad feelings do not need to disrupt our lives. There is help for every problem. Identify sources of help for yourself and for your friends and use them. (The group leader should have available a list of school and community resources.)

After this session, the leader should refer any student who is considered at risk to the school counselor or other mental health professional for follow-up. Some students may want to participate in the school's loss and grief support group, if one is available.

Non-Suicide Student Death

This session is similar to the one above, but the focus is not on suicide as the cause of death. If students do not know the facts regarding the student's death, relate these now. Ask if anyone has additional information, but discourage speculation and rumors.

1. Have students identify themselves by first name and tell how they knew this student. Students can share how they learned about the death, the last time they saw the student, or one thing they remember about the deceased. Go around the circle and ask questions to encourage participation, beginning with a student who is likely to share openly. (If the first student declines to answer, often others will follow this example.) State that it is all right to "pass" on any question.

2. If students talk freely, simply reflect their feelings while reinforcing the idea that it is good to experience our feelings. Identifying and experiencing feelings represents healthy versus unhealthy grieving.

3. If students do not talk freely, or after their initial sharing, ask the following questions:

- If you could ask (name of student who died) just one question now, what would it be?
- If you could say one thing to him or her now, what would it be?
- What are you feeling right now about this loss?—anger, resentment, fear, sadness, loneliness, confusion, guilt? Reinforce the naturalness of these feelings.

Some students feel guilt over previous thoughts or actions concerning the student who died.

4. Ask students what other deaths they have experienced and process their feelings. Ask "Who," "when," and "how" questions. Other

helpful questions include: "How did this person's death affect you? Were your feelings similar to or different from what you are feeling now?" The group leader should be aware that some students will suffer *rebound grief*—that is, they are not upset as much about *this* death as they are about an earlier death of someone close (Crenshaw, 1990, pp. 26–28, 109). When a classmate dies, students often get in touch with unresolved grief from previous losses.

5. Give students information about the stages of grief recovery and suggest coping strategies. Refer those who need further assistance to a loss and grief support group.

Teacher Death

This guide assumes that students know the facts regarding the teacher's death. If they do not, give this information, then proceed as follows.

1. Have students introduce themselves by first name and tell the group how they knew the teacher (e.g., a student in her or his class or member of a club the teacher sponsored). State that this news has made us sad, but sharing what we are feeling can help.

2. Ask students to identify what they are feeling. Some common responses are anger, fear, loneliness, confusion, emptiness, and guilt. *Frequently students feel guilty if they said or thought something negative about the teacher before her death.* Encourage students to discuss their feelings, pointing out similarities. If no one brings up the feeling of guilt, mention that feeling guilty is common after a teacher dies— it is a normal reaction. Students may need to forgive themselves for previous thoughts and actions.

3. If students talk freely, simply reflect their feelings while reinforcing the idea that it is good to experience feelings, even painful ones. Identifying and experiencing feelings represents healthy versus unhealthy grieving.

4. If students do not talk freely (or after their initial sharing) use these questions, asking for volunteers to reply:

- How did you learn about the death? (Students often want to tell how they heard.)
- What is one thing you remember about this teacher?
- If you could say one thing to her or him now, what would it be?
- What are some ways we might honor the memory of this teacher?

- Is this the first time someone close to you has died? Who died and how was the experience for you? How were your feelings similar to or different from what you are feeling now?

The group leader should be aware that some students will experience *rebound grief*—that is, they are not upset as much about this death as they are about an earlier death of someone close (Crenshaw, 1990, pp. 26–28, 109). When a teacher dies, students often get in touch with unresolved grief from the death of another adult in their lives.

5. Give students information about the stages of grief recovery and suggest coping strategies. Let students know that in the following weeks they may become angry easily or feel depressed, and that these reactions are common when grieving. Refer students who need further assistance to a loss and grief support group or a counseling professional for follow-up.

GUIDE FOR A MULTIPLE-SESSION SUPPORT GROUP

Unfortunately most support groups are begun only when a tragic death affects many students. A school with a proactive, developmental guidance program doesn't wait for a tragedy, but schedules groups periodically for students who are grieving the death of a parent, sibling, other relative, or close friend. A school that has personnel trained in grief facilitation and offers loss and grief support groups routinely is better prepared to respond effectively when a tragic death occurs.

An eight-session support group is outlined below, but the number of sessions a leader chooses to offer will vary depending on students' ages and grade levels. Some counselors need nine or more sessions to cover all the material; others, by omitting a number of the suggested activities, need fewer sessions. Although the use of a video is mentioned as an activity in one or more sessions, using a video is not essential to a group's success. The content of the support group is guided by the needs of the students. In each session there is usually a learning portion and a sharing portion, but these segments are integrated and fluid rather than separate entities. Group goals and suggested topics for a support group are as follows:

Group Goals

- To identify losses (even those that are not obvious);
- To understand the grief recovery process;
- To share experiences and feelings related to a death; and
- To learn how to cope with loss.

Learning Portion

- Types of losses:
  Losses that are obvious—Someone dies. A student breaks up with his girlfriend, or his parents get divorced.
  Losses that are frequently overlooked—A student changes schools, her best friend moves, or she unexpectedly receives a low or failing grade. A student graduates, has a prized possession stolen, or is waiting for her boyfriend to call after a fight.
- Stages of grief recovery;
- Healthy versus unhealthy reactions; and
- How to recognize and cope with depression and anger.

Sharing Portion

- What we think and feel about our loss;
- Surviving loss and healing emotional wounds;
- How we are growing from our loss; and
- Saying good-bye to the one who died.

The group leader, based on his or her judgment of what the group needs at a particular time, may delete or modify activities and rearrange the order of the following outline. The leader may design other activities or choose some from suggestions in chapter 4. All groups are different—members share freely in some and need few structured activities; in other groups, the leader must provide more direction.

SESSION 1

Leaders should prepare for this session by reading about the stages of grief recovery (viz. Colgrove et al., 1976; Crenshaw, 1990; Jewett, 1982; Tatelbaum, 1980).

1. Introduce the group leader(s).
2. Explain how the group will be structured, noting that there will be time for learning and for sharing.
3. Discuss limits of confidentiality and group guidelines.
   - **Group members** will not discuss outside the group what others say or do in the group.
   - **Group leaders** will hold in confidence what students say or do in the group, with the exception of anything indicating that a member may harm her- or himself or others.

- Group members will be respectful and listen to one another.
- Although sharing about loss is an important step in grief recovery, students may "pass" on any activity or question.
4. Ask group members if they think these rules are reasonable and important and if they will abide by them.
5. **Sharing Portion**. Have group members introduce themselves and share briefly the details of the death they are grieving: Who died and how? How were they related? How did they learn about the death? What did they think or feel at the time of the death? Relate these feelings to the initial stage of shock and denial. Discuss the commonality of group members' feelings and experiences. (Yalom [1985] discussed "universality" and other curative factors that operate in counseling groups.)
6. **Learning Portion**. Present information about the stages of grief recovery. Three simplified stages are:
   - **Shock and Denial:** ("I can't believe she's dead! . . . This can't be happening.")
   - **Anger/Depression:** ("The doctor should have known he couldn't survive another surgery." "I really feel awful. I'll never find another friend like her.")
   - **Acceptance/Resolution:** ("It's been hard, but I know now that I can go on." "I can't live in the past; I must look to the future.").

   Explain that the time one remains in each stage depends on the seriousness of the loss. Recovery from the death of someone close may take a long time. (Note: If the sharing portion takes all the available time, the leader can present the learning portion at the next session.)
7. For closure, have students state: "When _____ died, my first thoughts were _____."

SESSION 2

1. Review (or present) the stages of grief recovery, stressing that we grieve *minor* losses as well as major ones. Have volunteers relate a minor loss they have experienced, how they felt immediately after the loss, and after some time had passed; or ask, "Have you ever turned in an assignment or quiz thinking you did very well, only to have it returned with a low grade?" (Most students can relate to this.) Ask what they felt or thought when they looked at the grade. (*Shock and Denial*: "I can't believe it! . . . This must not be my paper.") And what did they do or say next? (*Anger/Depression*: "The teacher didn't tell

us this would be on the test!" or "I should have studied more! I really feel awful.") What next? (*Acceptance/Resolution:* "Oh, well, I'll do better next time." "It's only a quiz, not my whole grade!")

2. Ask students to share details about the person who died or their feelings related to the death. Encourage group members to ask questions as others share. (The group should not become a conversation between the leader and the student who is sharing. If the group has more than seven members, have students share in dyads.) Often students talk about guilt, anger, inability to cry, or how others reacted to their crying. Some believe that they are already in the final stage of recovery. Use items 3, 4, or 5 below as appropriate, or discuss "magical thinking" that leads to guilt feelings. (Note: Only some of these activities can be included in any *one* session. Those omitted are included in later sessions as the group leader deems appropriate.)

3. Read the first two pages and the first paragraph of the third page in *The Courage to Grieve* (Tatelbaum, 1980). Stress that although recovery from a major loss can take a very long time, the quickest path to recovery is *grieving fully at the time of the loss*. State that this group will provide members an opportunity to recall the loss and experience feelings they did not process fully at the time of the death. Emphasize that progress through the stages of recovery is more like a lightning bolt than a beam of light—those who grieve have good as well as bad days as their emotional wounds heal.

4. Ask students to think about who cried when their loved one or friend died. Who did not cry? What did people say to those who were crying? How did this feel? Have students share their answers and then give examples of times when they were uncomfortable when someone cried or when others were uncomfortable because they themselves were crying. Have students discuss what they have learned about crying from their parents or others. Point out that (a) crying is healthy; (b) crying is one way our body heals itself after an emotional wound; and (c) each person has his or her own reason for not wanting to cry. Give students a copy of the following excerpt from *The Courage to Grieve* (Tatelbaum, 1980).* Have each student read one of the statements.

> If you cry, I might cry.
> If you cry, I might know I too am in pain.
> If you cry, I might feel self-conscious about my own difficulty in crying.
> If you cry, I might have to face the unpleasantness in my/your life.

---

*Excerpt from *The Courage to Grieve* by Judith Tatelbaum. Copyright© 1980 by Judith Tatelbaum. Reprinted by permission of Harper Collins Publishers.

> If you cry, I might not be able to maintain my pose of strength
> (or dignity, or composure, or whatever).
> If you cry, I might cry for all the pain in my own life and never
> stop crying.
> Therefore, if you cry, I will have to run away or shut you up to
> save myself. (p. 77)

Ask, "Which of these is the reason you don't like to cry?" (If students are reluctant to share, the leader can tell which applies to him or her personally.)

5. Say, "We have talked about feeling shock, anger, and depression after a loss. Another commonly felt emotion is *fear*. What was scary or still frightens you when you of think this death?"

6. State that identifying exactly *what* we lost as a result of a death (e.g., "someone who thought I was great; my cheerleader; someone I could really talk to; someone to take me fishing; the chance to be a big brother"), can help resolve our grief. Discuss or have students write a reaction to this statement: "When _____ died I lost _____." Collect the papers and add comments. (See page 28 for examples of leader comments.)

7. Ask students to bring a picture of the person who died to the next session. Those who do not have a picture can draw a picture or write a description of the person.

SESSION 3

1. Have students show their pictures and introduce the person who died. Model by saying: "This is my father who died in February of 1975. He was 62 years old and . . . ." It is important that the group members begin to use the word *died* in place of euphemisms (e.g., went away, passed, was lost), which keep grievers in denial. Use dyads for this activity if there are more than seven group members.

2. Show a video (optional activity), appropriate to the students' grade level, that fosters an understanding of the grief process or helps students explore their feelings about death and dying. One video, *Dying is Part of Living*, parts 1 and 2, may be used in this session for middle and high school students. *As We Learn to Fall: A Look at Death and Grief and Coping and Living* can be used in grades 4 to 12, and *Blackberries in the Dark*, based on the novel by Mavis Jukes (1985), is appropriate for grades 4 to 6. The group leader should preview videos carefully. (Several videos are described briefly in Appendix A.) Before the video begins, state that viewers often find that films make them sad. Encourage students not to be afraid to express their feelings. Shedding tears, rather than denying sad feelings, is an important part of the recovery process.

3. Have students answer questions from a study guide that accompanies the video or one designed by the leader (see sample below). Discuss the answers and other points that group members raise.

4. Return reaction papers from the previous session and allow a few minutes for students to read the leader's comments. Ask volunteers to share their statements with the group. Discuss how "understanding and finishing with loss hinges on our admitting *what* we lost. Knowing precisely what is now gone enables us to grieve fully and perhaps fill that gap in the future" (Tatelbaum, 1980, p. 111). Ask students if they can identify another person to provide what they lost: "How can this need be met by others or by some action *you* can take?"

5. For closure, have each student give two words that describe how they are feeling or state one thing they have learned from this group. Ask students to bring their photos to the next session. (Or the leader may keep the photos and bring them to the next session.)

Sample Study Guide for Video Presentation

1. List some of the emotions the main character(s) experiences after the death.

2. Notice how he or she passes through each stage of grief recovery that we have discussed.

3. What is "magical thinking" or a "mortality crisis" (*or other concepts addressed in the video*)?

4. Who was most helpful to the grieving young person? What did he or she do that was helpful?

(Continue with other questions appropriate to the selected video. A list of suggested readings may be given as a handout.)

SESSION 4

If parts 1 and 2 of the video *Dying is Part of Living* were shown in the previous session, part 3 can be used in this session. The leader, however, should learn about hospice programs (Magno, 1990) and the

Kübler-Ross (1969) stages related to the anticipation of one's own death discussed in this video.

1. If some students did not share *what they lost* at the last session, give them an opportunity to do so now. Continue with item 2 below or other activities omitted in previous sessions.

2. Instruct students to close their eyes, sit quietly for a few minutes, and think about what the deceased would say about them—"How would this person describe you?" After a few minutes, have students show the picture of the one who died and "become that person," who then describes the student. For example, Jose becomes his deceased grandfather and says, "I am Jose Garza's grandfather. Jose is very special to me. He is a good student. I really like to take him fishing with me." (**Note:** This exercise can be powerful, and students may experience intense emotional pain. Students should not be required to participate, and leaders should not use the exercise unless they are comfortable with intense grief reactions.)

3a. When using part 3 of the video *Dying is Part of Living* , review the stages of grief recovery and explain how they are similar to, yet different from, the stages of coping in anticipation of one's own death. Show the video and discuss members' reactions.

3b. If the video is not used, continue with activities that seem appropriate and have not been used in prior sessions. Some activities described in chapter 4 (e.g., the metaphors, "loss-line," or "family constellation") may be used in this session.

4. For closure, have students share one feeling they experienced today, or one thing in particular they learned.

SESSION 5

This session is sometimes omitted, but is effective when the group meets prior to a major holiday. Before the session, the leader should learn about depression, especially as it affects children and adolescents (Lobel & Hirschfeld, 1984).

Depression in General

1. To generate a list of the symptoms of depression ask, "How do we know when a person is depressed? What does the person do, say, and look like?" Add additional symptoms from your knowledge. (If you, the leader, have ever been depressed, you may want to share how you felt.) Ask about depression these students have felt since the death. Discuss some causes of depression.

- *Biological makeup*—Some people seem physiologically disposed to depression. A chemical or endocrine imbalance or a serious illness can cause depression.

- *Life events*—When someone suffers a great loss (e.g., a loved one dies, a home burns down, or parents get a divorce), he or she may become depressed. And the depression may return on the anniversary of the event. Point out that there is a difference, however, in feeling sad as we often do, and a deep depression that doesn't go away.
- *Old age*—Older people become depressed more frequently than the young (related to life events).
- *Medications*—Some drugs cause depression (e.g., high blood pressure medicines, hormones, steroids, and certain anticancer agents).
- *Personality type*—People who are highly self-critical, very demanding, or passive and dependent are prone to suffer depression. People who have difficulty expressing their anger may become depressed.

2. Ask, "What do you do when you become depressed? What can we do to be helpful to a friend, parent, or relative who becomes depressed?" Discuss strategies that help including these:

- Talk to a friend, teacher, or counselor about what is causing the depression when it follows some "life event."
- If there is no apparent reason for the depression, try to identify an event (or person) that made you angry or disappointed you recently. It may be that you are holding in anger or feelings of disappointment that should be expressed. There are ways to release strong feelings even if you don't want to confront the person involved. One is to write a letter about your feelings. You may mail the letter, throw it away, or burn it. You don't have to express your anger directly to the person involved.
- Because depression is often the result of a *loss*, try to identify the loss. Remind students that their losses aren't always obvious: Earning a lower grade than expected on a quiz was, perhaps, more disappointing than you thought. Waiting to hear about something important—*"Will my Dad be here for my birthday?"* or *"Are we really going to move?"*—can feel like a loss. Talk to someone about your feelings.
- Get some physical exercise! Studies (Hopson, 1988) indicate that exercise raises the level of endorphins (*en-door-fins*) in the brain, which in turn makes us feel more positive and decreases sad feelings. Endorphins are natural "up-

pers," responsible for the feelings some refer to as a "runner's high."

- If depression is severe or just won't let up, see a medical doctor and ask to be checked for clinical depression. Such depression usually does not go away without special treatment.

- Seek professional counseling, and if friends or close relatives become severely depressed, insist that they get help. Students should seek assistance from teachers or a counselor for a severely depressed friend or classmate. Never take lightly another person's hints or outright expressions of a desire to die (e.g., *"I just want go to sleep and never wake up;" "Everyone would be better off without me;"* or similar expressions). These may be signs of deep depression and are **always a cry for help**.

Depression During Holidays

1. Ask students if they know someone who becomes depressed at holiday times. Feeling depressed during holidays is common. Celebrating a holiday without a loved one is especially hard the first year or two following the death. Young people need to understand these feelings to help themselves or others (e.g.,their parents) who become depressed. Ask, "What are other reasons we may become depressed at this usually happy time of year?" (Answers may include trying to do too much or not having enough money.) Young people, in particular, become depressed for the following reasons:

- In a *blended family*, traditions may be different from those observed when they lived with both of their own parents.
- Due to a divorce or a family move, students may not see a parent or friends from their previous home town.
- Family tensions are often greater around holidays, and children may receive more negative input from parents.

2. For closure, have students share what they will miss most on this holiday (or missed at the last major holiday) because of the death of their loved one or friend and describe one way they will cope with their sad feelings.

SESSION 6

This session may be omitted if none of the deaths was a suicide, but may be used sooner than session 6 if several deaths were suicides.

1. Give each student a copy of the Ann Landers column, "Counseling Works," reprinted on page 68. Have a male student read the first paragraph, then ask, "Do you think many teenagers feel this way?" Have another student read the second paragraph, then ask, "Have you ever felt that way? Can you think of a time when you were 'dying' inside and no one knew?" (Give students time to answer the questions covertly if no one shares aloud.) Have a volunteer read the third paragraph, then ask, "Do you think teenagers are good at hiding their sad feelings?" Have another student finish reading the letter.

The leader should read the poem, making sure students understand unfamiliar terms (e.g., *"crown"* = head; *"quietly arrayed"* = not a flashy dresser; *"in fine"* = in fact; *"cursed the bread"* = cursed our poverty; *"waited for the light"* = hoped for better times).

2. Ask students what they think Richard Cory was like. State that we don't really know, but will try to imagine. Was he young, old, married, single? Where did he live—in a mansion, a condo? What kind of job, if any, did he have? How did he get his "riches"? Ask, "How can we be rich, other than with money and worldly goods?" Discuss the following:

- What are some riches Richard Cory did not have?
- What finally brought him to take his life?
- How could we have helped him? Could the people who knew Richard Cory have prevented his death?

Explain that we cannot take responsibility for others' actions. We can be helpful, we can listen, and we can try to recognize when someone needs help. However, we cannot stay with others 24 hours a day, and we can't control their choices. Include points from the single-session group for a student suicide death outlined earlier in this chapter. (**Note:** Answers to the discussion questions above may reveal students' thoughts about themselves.)

3. If time permits, have students write a short reaction to one of the following:

- I *would* **not** have wanted to be Richard Cory's friend.
- I *would* have wanted to be Richard Cory's friend.

Collect the reaction papers and return them at the next session with comments.

4. For closure, have students share one thought about today's session. Ask students to bring their photos to the next session.

Ann Landers: "Counseling Works"

Dear Ann Landers: I am a male in my mid-30s and have been reading your column for many years. A recent letter about a teen-age suicide struck close to home. I, too, was considered the "perfect" son. I was good-looking, an excellent student, popular, did well in athletics and was an outstanding musician. Everyone thought I must be the happiest kid in the world. I really had it made.

Actually, I was a different person inside. Nobody knew of my fears and insecurities and the unhappy days and nights I covered up with a big smile and a lively sense of humor. More than once I considered suicide, but I couldn't bring myself to do it.

Your statement was so wise and insightful: "Sometimes the more cheerful a person appears, the more miserable he is. Facades can be so well-constructed it is impossible to tell what is behind them."

I decided at age 22 to get counseling. It saved my life. My therapist helped me verbalize my real feelings about myself and those close to me. It was terrific to express anxieties and hostilities that had been deeply buried for so many years.

I cut out a column you wrote many years ago because I saw myself. It made me decide to get professional help. Please run it again. It may do the same for someone else.—J., My Name Is Legion

Dear J.: Here it is. The author is Edwin Arlington Robinson (1869–1935).

Whenever Richard Cory went downtown,
We people on the pavement looked at him:
He was a gentleman from sole to crown,
Clean favored and imperially slim.
And he was always quietly arrayed,
And he was always human when he talked;
But still he fluttered pulses when he said,
"Good morning," and he glittered when he walked.
And he was rich—yes, richer than a king—
And admirably schooled in every grace:
In fine, we thought that he was everything

From "Counseling Works" by Ann Landers, 1983, *Chicago Tribune.* Permission granted by Ann Landers and Creators Syndicate. The poem "Richard Cory" is from *The Children of the Night* by Edwin Arlington Robinson (New York: Charles Scribner's Sons, 1987).

To make us wish that we were in his place.
So on we worked, and waited for the light,
And went without the meat, and cursed the bread;
And Richard Cory, one calm summer night,
Went home and put a bullet through his head.

SESSION 7

This outline, which should be used near the end (but not at the last session) of the group, involves writing a letter to the deceased. The purpose of this activity is to help students acknowledge the reality of their loss, identify their ambivalent feelings about the deceased, and to say good-bye "on an emotional rather than an intellectual level" (Crenshaw, 1990, p. 24). Many professionals in the field of grief counseling (viz. Crenshaw, chapter 1; James & Cherry, 1988, chapter 10; Kopp, 1983, pp. 51–65; Tatelbaum, 1980, chapter 12) have discussed the rationale for the letter's content outlined in point 2 below. Group leaders who study grief recovery theory will be better prepared to help students process the feelings that result from this activity.

1. Return reaction papers and ask who would have wanted to be Richard Cory's friend and who would *not* have wanted to be Richard Cory's friend. Discuss students' reasons.

2. Have students take out their pictures of the deceased, think about this person for a few minutes, and then write a letter to him or her using the outline below. Give students a copy of the outline and state that they may address some or all of the points.

- Tell what you remember about his death.
- Ask any questions you have related to the death or anything else that is puzzling to you.
- State what you wish you had said to this person before he or she died or that you wish you had said more often.
- List any regrets you may have about your relationship with this person. Make any apologies you think are necessary.
- Tell this person what you really liked or appreciated about him or her **and** how you wish he or she had been *different*.
- State specifically what you lost when this person died.
- Discuss the feelings you have had since the death and how your life is now.
- Discuss how you think your life would be different if he or she had not died.

Because some group members will finish sooner than others, take copies of *About Grief, a Scriptographic Booklet* (1990) or other books for students to read as they wait for others to finish.

3. To process this activity, ask, "How was this for you? What part was hardest to write? Why?" Then have volunteers read aloud all or parts of their letter. Because this experience can be painful, do not require students to participate. If the group is large, have students share in dyads or triads. Although some students may decline to read their letter, some will ask another group member to read it aloud for them. Most students, even if they do not share their letters, will respond to questions posed by the leader. For example, "How do you think that your life would be different today if _____ were alive?" Take up the letters and return them at the next session with your comments.

4. If time permits, add an activity omitted from prior sessions or discuss information from the scriptographic booklet.

5. If the next session will be the last, begin to facilitate closure to the group experience. You may have students tell one thing about the group that has helped them, or review different kinds of losses. If group discussions have centered on deaths, point out other losses that students frequently experience (e.g., parents' divorce, moving, or ending a romantic relationship). Emphasize that we grieve to some degree after each loss.

SESSION 8

This session may have a different number depending on how often the group meets. Previous outlines frequently cover more than one session, and some may have been omitted.

1. Return letters to group members and allow time for them to read the leader's comments. Ask for volunteers to read portions of their letters or share thoughts and feelings they have experienced since writing the letter.

2. Review the group experience using ideas similar to point 5 in the previous session outline.

3. Have each group member, in turn, receive feedback from others in the group. For example, each member tells Eve what he or she appreciates about her (or learned from her) and gives her encouragement or affirmations. Then group members do the same for Louis.

The group leader can prepare and duplicate a list of affirming statements. The list is then cut into small pieces, leaving one statement on each slip of paper. Several statements are given to each group member, who then chooses a statement to give to other group members. Examples of encouraging statements can be found in *How to Survive the Loss of a Love* (Colgrove et al., 1976): "You're stronger now, you've dealt with an experience of loss and have grown from it." "Heal at your own pace, don't be rushed by others." "Your anger will go away as your hurt heals." "You require time to heal. Give yourself the luxury. You deserve it."

3. Review the following points and ask group members for their comments:

- Psychological or emotional pain, like physical pain, has a beginning, a middle, and an end. Bad feelings do end. Your pain will heal.
- Even minor losses cause us to grieve. When feeling angry or depressed for no apparent reason, try to identify a loss you may have suffered, but did not allow yourself to grieve.
- There are several stages in the grief process (shock, denial, anger, depression, acceptance, understanding, reorganization, and resolution), and we cannot skip any of these. We must have our sad feelings, tears, and anger on the way to resolution. The grieving process takes **time!**
- Do not try to face a loss alone now or in the future—talk with a parent, a trusted friend, a teacher, or counselor. Although this group is ending, your school counselor will meet with you individually if you need further assistance.
- Sometimes reading books about grief can help us process our feelings or gain a healthy perspective about our loss. (Provide a reading list.)

4. Have each member complete an evaluation form (see Appendix B). Although the evaluation should be completed anonymously, the leader may request verbal feedback from volunteers.

LOGISTICS OF LEADING GROUPS

Before starting a group, the leader should secure administrative approval and support. If the principal strongly approves the activity, other personnel will usually be supportive, or at least cooperative. To gain the principal's support, the leader must have a well-defined plan for the group and show how group goals and objectives complement those of the school as a whole. Teachers should be informed about the goals and purposes of the group through in-service meetings or printed material. To be well prepared to facilitate healthy grieving, the leader must plan each session carefully and become knowledgeable about the topic to be discussed. A meeting room that allows for privacy should be scheduled and equipment and supplies (including boxes of tissue) arranged for well in advance of each session. Finding an appropriate meeting room, notifying students and their teachers, and getting students released from class for group sessions can be difficult; however, the results of an effective grief support group will justify the effort.

Scheduling Group Sessions

In secondary schools with multiple class periods, groups are scheduled to meet once or twice a week on a rotating class-period basis. For example, the first session is scheduled for the first period of the day, the next session for the second period, and so on. In this way, if group members have seven classes, they miss each class only once for a seven-session group. If schools have time scheduled each week for group or club meetings, this time can be utilized. In most schools, meeting with students before or after school is not feasible due to transportation problems. In elementary schools, the counselor works with individual teachers to determine when and where the group will meet.

Selecting Group Members

Following a death that affects a large segment of the student body, referrals for grief support groups come from teachers, students, administrators, and parents. When a group is scheduled routinely (i.e., not just following a tragic death), the group leader can ask teachers, administrators, and attendance clerks to refer students who have experienced a death. Groups can be advertised through flyers or stories in the school newspaper. After prospective group members are identified, the group leader will interview them to determine if their needs are appropriate for the group. The leader asks about the death, how the student is coping, and whether or not he is in therapy. Students currently in therapy with other professionals should be included only if their therapist approves. Even if a student is not in therapy, she may be excluded if the leader believes that she needs more in-depth treatment than is available in a school-based support group. The Grief Resolution Inventory (see Appendix B) can be used to determine where a student is in terms of grief resolution. This inventory can also serve as a pregroup and postgroup measure to evaluate the group experience as a means of helping students resolve their grief. In addition to interviewing students, the leader gives information about the structure and content of the group, the number of sessions, and group member responsibilities. If the group will have a closed format (i.e., members do not enter and leave at different times as in an "open" group), students who know that they will miss several sessions should not be included. All members need to be present for most sessions to foster group cohesion. Depending on grade level or age of the students and school policy, the leader may notify or have parents sign a group participation permission form for their child (see Appendix B).

Notifying Group Members and Teachers

Before a group begins, teachers should be told the date(s) a student will be absent from class for a group session. If the student will miss the class only once or twice, the leader will want to stress this fact. Often teachers are more supportive if they know that the student will miss the class only a few times. In elementary schools, the counselor usually makes personal contact with teachers of students who will participate in the group. Although the leader gives each group member a schedule of meeting times and dates at the first session, it may be necessary to send reminder notices or passes to students before each session. (See appendix B for sample notification forms.)

SUMMARY

Counselors, teachers, and administrators should work together to develop a support program to meet both routine and crisis needs of grieving students. The program may include classroom discussions, single-session group experiences, and ongoing grief support groups. Grief counseling with students following a tragic death in the school community helps resolve campuswide trauma. Support groups that are part of a developmental guidance program are also important because many students, throughout the school year, experience deaths that affect them personally. The information in this chapter and the case studies in the next chapter provide concrete examples of how counselors and teachers can assist grieving students.

■ CHAPTER 6 ■

Case Studies

Counselors and teachers are sought out in moments of confusion, pain, and grief. Recently new terms have been thrust before all of us for educational consideration: bereavement, death education, the grieving child. (Carroll, 1977)

Teachers and counselors who assist students and staff following a death learn much from these experiences. Case studies can add to the knowledge gained from personal experience by illustrating the application of certain principles and strategies. For those who lack personal experience, case studies provide a measure of realism to their study of theory and techniques. Four detailed case studies are included in this chapter. Two involve student suicides (one in which gang rivalry was an issue), one concerns the death of a student in an automobile accident, and another the homicide of a popular teacher. In addition, several short scenarios are given, followed by questions designed to stimulate thought about appropriate responses. Although all the cases are based on actual incidents, the names used are pseudonyms.

A STUDENT SUICIDE CAUSES CAMPUSWIDE TRAUMA

In early March 1986, a popular 17-year-old named Raul killed himself with a hunting rifle in a field near his home. Raul had been a member of the varsity football team and very active in one of the school's largest clubs at his 1,200-student, suburban high school. Many students, especially those who knew Raul well, were distressed and could not concentrate on normal school tasks. The counseling staff responded quickly to alleviate the trauma that was evident in a large portion of the student body.

Teachers were asked to read the following announcement to their first period classes:

The loss of a favorite pet or possession is often disturbing, and the loss of friends and familiar surroundings due to a move or to parents' separation or divorce is even more difficult. But the loss of a friend or relative through death is almost unbearable. You may feel depressed, sad, angry, lonely—or all of these things. How you work through these feelings and how you deal with your grief can be healthy or unhealthy.

You experience specific stages in the grieving process, but often need help in moving from one stage to another and in resolving your great sense of loss. The counseling staff will offer a group for students who need to deal with grief or a sense of loss at 12:30 P.M. Friday, in room 222. If you want to be part of the group (or want information about the group), you are welcome to attend.

Corporate Sharing

Expecting a group of 30 or 40 students, the counselors had arranged for one large room in which two counselors and the nurse would meet with the students in small groups. When over 400 students came, administrators quickly moved the group to the auditorium. A counselor addressed the group and acknowledged Raul's death and the sadness that everyone felt. Then, she gave some specific information and thoughts to help alleviate painful feelings, to give students permission to grieve, and to guard against other student suicides. The following points were presented:

- Almost everyone thinks about suicide at one time or another; it is not unnatural to do so.
- Suicidal thoughts are reactions to pain and despair, but there is no need to act on these thoughts. Anyone who feels that such thoughts are getting out of hand should seek help.
- A suicide attempt or a statement indicating a wish to die is always a cry for help—an attempt to communicate that "my life is unbearable; please help me out of this situation." What one really wants when hurting is not to get out of this world, but to get out of the present situation, to alleviate the pain.
- There is no one answer to "why" someone commits suicide; the answers are as varied as the individuals who make this unfortunate choice. Rather than dwelling on the "why," students can use their time better by learning how to recognize when someone may be suicidal and seeing that the person gets help.
- Emotional pain, like physical pain, has a beginning, a middle and an end—the bad feelings will heal. (Young people,

who have very little experience with grief reactions, often think that they will never be happy again.)

- Responses to grief vary (i.e., some people shed tears readily, others do not), and outward responses do not necessarily manifest the degree of grief one feels.
- Our "bad" thoughts or spoken words do not cause others to die. Likewise our "if only's" cannot change what has happened. We just are not that powerful!
- Feeling anger at the person who died, at God, or the world in general is normal when grieving.
- Feeling low or blue is a normal reaction to certain life experiences, as normal as feeling happy and hopeful. Bad feelings are a part of living, but they do not need to disrupt our lives.
- There is help for every problem. Identify sources of help for yourself and for your friends and use these resources when you are distressed.

Group Counseling

At the conclusion of the assembly, counselors invited the students who knew Raul personally and others who were very upset to participate in small group meetings. Three groups, each with about 25 students, met with counselors who used a common script to facilitate sharing. Students in the groups identified their feelings about Raul's death, cried, and responded to these questions:

- If you could ask Raul one question now, what would it be?
- If you could say one thing to Raul now, what would it be?
- What is your best memory of Raul?
- What is someone trying to say who attempts suicide?

Following the discussion, the counselor presented three simplified stages of grief recovery (i.e., 1. *Shock/Denial*, 2. *Anger/Depression*, and 3. *Acceptance/Resolution*) so that students would know what to expect in the weeks to come as they worked through their grief. The counselors announced that a series of small group counseling sessions would begin the following week and gave parent permission forms (see Appendix B) to those who wanted to participate.

Throughout the spring semester, 38 students met for seven sessions in four groups of 8 to 13 students each. Twenty-two of the participants were male and 16 were female. Group members included 7 ninth graders, 11 tenth graders, and 10 eleventh graders. Because this school had just opened, no 12th-grade students were enrolled. Some group members had learning disabilities and some were honor students. Each group session had a teaching/learning component and a sharing time similar to the outline presented in chapter 5. Instructional topics included the three stages of grief recovery, how to recognize when one needs to grieve and allowing oneself to do so, how to recognize and alleviate depression in oneself and others, and different types of loss. The group leader stressed that some losses are not obvious (e.g., making a poor test grade or losing a favorite piece of jewelry), yet all the stages of grief recovery must be mastered.

Initially the sharing portion centered on Raul's death, but soon students began to talk about other losses they had experienced—their parents' divorce, death of a parent, moving and leaving friends, breaking up with a girlfriend or boyfriend, and theft of personal belongings. Although several students had experienced the death of a parent or other close relative years ago, they had not worked through their grief.

Near the end of some sessions, the counselor asked students to write a reaction to a statement; for example, "*What specifically did you lose when _____ died (or when your parents divorced)?*" This technique provided students a private means of sharing painful feelings and increased the group leader's understanding of grieving teenagers. Students' responses included these: "**When my father died I lost** *the chance of growing up with someone to take me fishing and hunting like my friends have now. It makes me sad to hear them talk about what I will never have.*"

"**When my mother died I lost** *someone to talk to. Now that I am getting older and have all sorts of problems, I feel I have no one to turn to.*"

"**When Raul died I lost** *a sense of sureness in my life, like I could go any minute. Any of my friends could die, or my Mom.*"

"**When we moved I lost** *many friends who knew who I was . . . and I just feel like nobody here.*"

"**When Raul died I lost** *my will to care for anything as much as I have in the past. It seems as if right after something great happens, a bunch of little things follow and ruin it. So, why get excited about good happenings?!*"

The group leaders read what the students had written, added their comments, and returned the papers to the students at the next session. Students were given an opportunity to share their statements with the group. Some shared readily, but others did not—the thoughts and feeling they expressed in the reaction papers were too painful.

Evaluation

After the last session, the group leaders asked students to evaluate the group experience. Evaluation forms were completed by 32 (84%) of the participants. All 32 stated that they would recommend this type of group to other students and that they had grown in their understanding of the grief process and in their ability to share feelings. Listed below are representative statements from the evaluations:

One thing I have learned is: *"It's good to let your hurt out." ". . .to share my feelings . . ." ". . .how to cope with hurt and pain."*

When I began the group I thought: *"that no one would really listen to me." ". . . that I was going to be unhappy forever! " ". . . I wouldn't be able to talk about Raul's death."*

Now I feel: *"that I can handle losing a thing that means a lot to me." " . . . I can trust and talk more comfortably with people."*

The best thing about this group was: *"sharing your feelings without being afraid to cry." " . . .knowing you are not alone in your feelings. " ". . .that I learned to deal with loss."*

Students who participated in these loss and grief groups gained knowledge and skills to help themselves and others who experience a loss. The groups served both a responsive and a developmental purpose. (Note: Over 250 students have participated in grief support groups at this school in the past 6 years.)

Follow-Up

Before the school year ended, administrators and counselors provided information about how to recognize distressed or suicidal teens, how to make referrals, and strategies for helping vulnerable young people to all faculty and staff. As the faculty became alert to signs of despair in students, they shared with counselors a number of student comments and drawings they might have previously ignored. Students also referred to counselors their friends about whom they were concerned. The counseling staff held many teacher consultations, parent conferences, and individual counseling sessions.

A TEACHER HOMICIDE

The Tuesday morning headline read: *"Teacher Killed in Store Robbery"* (Lane, 1991). But in this well-established community, located just beyond the downtown area of a large city, many people knew of the death before this headline shattered their usually peaceful world. Several neighbors had stood crying outside the store in disbelief shortly after the shooting the night before. The 46-year-old victim, Mr. Lee Wong, was a middle school history and physical education teacher. As an assistant coach for the football, basketball, and track teams, he was well known and respected. Mr. Wong had been enrolled in master's degree courses at a local university. Because of this added expense, he had taken a part-time job at a neighborhood convenience store. Ironically, he had decided just a few days before his death to give up this part-time job that gave him little time for his family.

Realizing from experience that the trauma within the student body would be extensive, the staff person in charge of crisis intervention set in motion the school district's response plan. The plan utilized district-level staff, the school's counselors and teachers, and counselors from other campuses.

Group Counseling

The day after Mr. Wong's death, 12 counselors from throughout the district came to the middle school campus to help grieving students and staff. Several were from the elementary schools these students had previously attended, thus providing familiar faces. Almost half the 1,080 students at the school came to the library to meet with counselors individually and in small groups. Most were tearful, some were nearly hysterical, and others quietly grieved this senseless death. The crisis intervention specialist and the school's coaches counseled the football team in the locker room. This large group of boys was divided into smaller groups, and their coaches helped them process their feelings. As counseling groups continued throughout the day, students and staff had many questions: "Why Mr. Wong? Why this violent murder? Why did it have to happen this way? It's not fair—why him?" The halls were unusually quiet for a middle school campus.

Other Activities

In classrooms and counseling sessions, teachers and counselors encouraged students to talk or write about their feelings or complete art activities using supplies gathered from the art classroom. Some students wrote long letters to Mr. Wong and his family, and others made sympathy cards from colored paper and paints. One young man wrote, "I am sorry for your husband's death. I loved the man and so did the rest of our team. He helped us . . . with advice on how to improve." Boxes were placed in hallways to collect expressions of sympathy that students wanted delivered to the family.

As another outlet for their feelings, students wrote messages or made drawings on 10-foot long sheets of butcher paper posted on walls inside and outside the school. These sheets (10 in all), filled with comments, good-byes, accolades, and colorful tributes, were taken to the funeral home and given to the teacher's family. Some messages read: "We will miss you. We love you. You're number one!"

Many students were still upset as school recessed, and their parents were deeply concerned. The school remained open that evening, and community mental health professionals, ministers, priests, and school counselors met with distraught parents and students. Despite the sadness, there was a sense of the community pulling together in this great tragedy.

Many current and former students were among the 1,000 people who attended the funeral the following afternoon. Football team members wore their red and white school jerseys, and the cheerleaders wore their uniforms. Other students held red and white balloons on which they had written farewell messages. They released the balloons at the grave site of this man who had meant so much to them and to the community.

Follow-Up

Some students at the school needed counseling for weeks, and a few were referred to community mental health agencies. The crisis team and school staff met to "debrief" and to plan strategies for the next crisis, all the while hoping that they would never have to use them.

STUDENT SUICIDE SPARKS GANG VIOLENCE

On Wednesday morning in early September of 1991, a secretary in the Office of Student Support Services (in an urban district serving 65,000 students) heard a radio report concerning a suicide. She immediately notified the district's crisis coordinator, who called the police department to verify the facts. The police reported that an 18-year-old had shot himself and was on life-support at a local hospital. The police department in this progressive Southern city usually notifies the Office of Student Support Services about student deaths or injuries. However, because this victim was 18 years old, police investigators assumed he was not a student and did not contact district personnel.

Crisis Team Leader Coordinates Response

The young man, named Chester, was well known and admired by many students at his 2,000-student high school. Some of Chester's teachers had worked hard to help him succeed. The news of his suicide attempt shocked administrators, teachers, and students alike. The crisis coordinator called the principal and proceeded to the high school to coordinate the response plan. Students who quickly learned of the shooting were upset, shocked, and depressed. Some students became increasingly angry as the day went by.

Unusual Factors Complicate the Grief Process

The crisis coordinator taught two of the classes in which Chester had been enrolled at the request of the teacher who was herself grieving. Over 100 students came for individual and group counseling. Several factors complicated the grief process, for example:

- Many students would not accept Chester's death until he was taken off life-support later in the afternoon.
- Chester had been a leader of the "REDS" gang, and his death was seen as an attempt to escape gang involvement. (A recent news report quoted Chester as saying that his only alternatives were death or jail.)
- Students still remembered the tragic suicide of one of their fellow students during the previous school year.

Because of their acute grief reactions and secrets and fears related to gang involvement, many students were reluctant to share their thoughts or feelings in group sessions. The large number of students seeking help made it difficult to provide small group and one-to-one counseling. When counselors did meet with students individually, the counseling was more productive.

Gang Rivalry: A Factor in Campus Tension

The school principal and crisis team leader met with the faculty after the school day ended. Teachers were provided information to use in their classrooms the next day to assist grieving students. The principal, counselors, and many teachers in this school had prior experience with student suicide and knew how to help students; however, the element of gang rivalry provided new challenges. There were reports of increasing anger among "REDS" members and their girlfriends over remarks rival gang members were making about Chester. A rumor was circulating that a gang fight would erupt after school. A gang-related shooting did occur that evening, and a ranking member of a rival gang was injured from a gunshot.

Crisis counseling with students continued throughout the next day. Two special education staff members, a school nurse, a counseling intern, and several community volunteers assisted the school's counselors. Students talked about their pain, anger, and fear of gang retaliation. Tension on campus increased when Chester's picture was posted on lockers of rival gang members. However, most students behaved responsibly, and the student body seemed reassured by the high level of security on campus and the fact that those involved in the shooting the previous night were not at school.

The crisis coordinator was busy throughout the day supervising the counseling efforts, working with suicidal students, checking on rumors, relaying facts, and keeping in contact with the local police department. There were rumors that rival gang members might retaliate with drive-by shootings at Chester's wake Sunday night or at the funeral Monday.

Recommendations

Several unusual factors made this student's suicide more difficult for the crisis intervention team than previous student suicides. After reviewing the interventions used, the crisis coordinator made recommendations to improve future responses to deaths that affect a school campus:

- Train more crisis counselors who can be deployed to district schools when a crisis occurs.
- Designate an alternate or assistant crisis team leader who can be called on when the crisis coordinator is not available or when multiple crises occur. (Several callers had requested assistance from the Office of Student Support Services while the staff was involved with this crisis.)
- Provide portable communication devices (walkie-talkies) to simplify communication between counselors in the counseling rooms, the crisis team leader, and administrators during a campus crisis.
- In any future deaths of gang members, do *not* use the name given the student by his or her gang when talking with other students. Doing so tends to exacerbate gang rivalry.
- Establish "punching bag areas" in all high schools where students can go to work off anger and frustration. Hostile students can use these areas during a crisis to vent their emotions without harming themselves or others.
- Provide in-service training for all teachers (*before* a tragedy occurs) on how to respond to grief reactions in their classrooms and how to identify students who are a high risk for suicide.
- Initiate student assistance programs on all campuses (e.g., peer helpers or special counselors) to address special needs of students throughout the year and in times of crisis.
- Assist the local police department in facilitating a gang "summit" to allow rival members to make peace yet save face.
- Develop a more comprehensive plan and system of coordination to deal with gangs in schools.

ACCIDENTAL DEATH OF A STUDENT

Just after midnight on a Saturday morning in February 1992, a car occupied by three teenage girls veered off the roadway to avoid a speeding car that approached with its headlights off. Their car was demolished when it hit a large tree, throwing the 17-year-old driver and a 14-year-old passenger from the vehicle. A 15-year-old girl was trapped inside where she died within the hour. Emergency medical personnel transported the two critically injured girls to local hospitals.

Confirming the Death

According to news reports, Maria Leal (the girl who died) and 14-year-old Lori Herrington, one of the injured, were enrolled at the same high school. Local newspapers had reported Maria's death, but conflicting information surfaced about whether or not the younger girl had died at the hospital. One report stated that she had died Sunday afternoon. Sunday night the principal called the counselor who usually coordinates the school's response following a death to discuss a tentative action plan. The principal had scheduled a meeting of key staff for 8:00 A.M. Monday. However, because response plans would depend on whether there had been one or two deaths, the principal wanted to confirm the younger girl's death. When he called the hospital, he learned that Lori was still alive; the report of her death was erroneous. The principal then called the counselor to relay this information. Sunday night the counselor prepared an announcement about Maria's death, memos for teachers of the injured student, and outlines that could be followed in counseling groups of grieving students. The school had used similar information sheets after previous student deaths, and these scripts were stored in the counselor's personal computer. The principal notified key staff members to meet at the school at 8:00 A.M. on Monday.

Key Personnel Consider Appropriate Action

At the Monday morning meeting of administrators, counselors, and department heads, more conflicting information surfaced. The name of the injured student, Lori Herrington, was not in student data files at this 2,200-student high school. Although her address was in this school's attendance area, her name was not familiar to staff members. A counselor called the number in the local telephone book for Lori's last name and address (this information was in news reports), but a recording stated that this was a nonworking number. The planning group assumed that the injured student had probably moved from the school's attendance area and was not enrolled.

It was important to determine the degree of trauma that could be expected campuswide because all the school's counselors were scheduled to be in classrooms most of the day conducting a career development program. These activities could be rescheduled if the staff believed that many students would be affected. Based on the schema discussed in chapter 2 (see page 21), the staff decided that the impact on the school as a whole would be minimal. Maria was not well known (which yielded a value of 3) and the death, which occurred in the local community (a value of 2), had been accidental (a value of 3). Because the funeral was scheduled for the afternoon and her close friends probably would not be at school, the "degree of trauma" total was reduced by 1 point. The staff decided that the death would be discussed with Maria's classmates, but not announced schoolwide. Although the career development program continued, one counselor (who had experience in loss and grief counseling) was relieved of this assignment to be available to students who might need assistance.

The Response Plan

The school counselor, who led the school's grief support groups each year, went to Maria's first period class to let her classmates know about the death and to process their feelings. From students in this class, the counselor learned that the injured student, Lori Herrington, was enrolled, but under her legal name, Lorene Smith. The confusion resulted from the fact that this student frequently used the name "Lori" (which she preferred to Lorene) and, when not in school, she used her stepfather's last name of Herrington. With this information, the counselor secured a copy of Lori's schedule and notified her teachers about the accident.

Throughout the day the counselor went to each class in which Maria had been enrolled. She gave a factual account of the accident and asked if anyone had information to add. After addressing the students' comments and questions, the counselor proceeded with these thoughts:

> It is sad and sometimes frightening when a classmate dies. It makes us realize that bad things can happen to people we know—they can get into accidents, they can die. We expect older people to die, and we frequently hear about deaths of young people we don't know. But when it happens to someone we know, someone we saw everyday, it's scary. We know that we or someone we love also could have an accident.

She continued:

> How many of you have experienced the death of someone close? (pause) Quite a few, I see. I'm sure you agree that nothing really

prepares us for the death of someone close. We see death every-
day on television and in the movies or we read about it, but
these experiences do not prepare us for the actual event. There
are things you can do, however, when you are grieving—talk to
a trusted friend, relative, or school counselor; write about your
feelings; do something for someone else who is hurting. When
someone we love dies, our memories and the memories that
others share with us are special. If you would like to write to
Maria's family, I know your memories of her would be welcome.
Your teacher will allow time now for you to write a letter, or if
you prefer, a paragraph or two about what you are thinking or
feeling about this death. If you want your letter delivered, give
it to your teacher. Does anyone have a question or comment
before I leave? . . . If you want to talk with a counselor either
now or later today, ask your teacher for a pass to the counseling
office.

Some students were more distressed than others, and some classes
were particularly responsive. Several students came to the counseling
office and were counseled individually or in small groups. One boy
named Ralph (whose mother had died the previous February) left his
classroom after hearing about his classmate's death and smashed his
fists into a locker located nearby. He was taken to the nurse's office
and later had a long conference with his counselor. Ralph was suffering
rebound grief (Crenshaw, 1990, pp. 26–28). Hearing about this death
brought back the feelings he had experienced when his mother died.
The counselor called Ralph's aunt, who reported that Ralph had been
depressed for about 2 weeks, a common reaction to the first anniversary
of a loved one's death. The counselor gave the aunt several referrals
to community resources and suggested that Ralph might profit from
seeing a therapist.

Toward the end of the day, the principal used the public address
system to call for a moment of silence in memory of the student who
died. Some of Maria's friends had requested that the principal play a
special song after the silent tribute. The principal, however, denied the
request. The rationale for his decision was twofold—first, the school
had not played songs after previous deaths; and second, the music could
evoke strong emotions just before school ended when students would
be leaving campus and not have the support of teachers and counselors.

Debriefing

The school staff learned several things from this experience. First, it
is essential to check and recheck information related to a reported
death. Second, based on the limited impact this death had on the
student body, the decision to forego a schoolwide announcement (other

than the memorial moment of silence) seemed warranted. Third, because a fatal accident or violent death of a student is more likely to occur on weekends, classroom or other activities that take counselors away from their offices should not be scheduled on Mondays.

OTHER CASES

After reading the cases that follow, take a few minutes to decide what actions should be taken immediately and in the following weeks and months. Then, answer the questions specific to each case. Refer to other chapters for assistance in formulating your plans and answers. Additional information about the response plan that was followed in some of these cases is available in the references cited.

A shooting occurs in a second-grade classroom. On a sunny morning in May, a woman with a long history of psychological problems walked into a Chicago area elementary school and opened fire on a class of second graders. One child died and five others were seriously wounded. As the woman fled the school, the teachers and administrators of this suburban school assisted the frightened children. Emergency medical personnel rushed the injured students to a local hospital. Many students in other parts of the building were unaware of the shooting, but some parents began arriving when they heard about the incident.

1. Who will address these parents, and what information will they be given?

2. What actions may be necessary to make students feel that their school is safe?

A sixth-grade suicide stuns a small school. Jim was one of nine sixth graders enrolled in a very small private school located in the suburbs of a major city. "He had argued with his best friend and classmate, Bob, on Friday over a secret Jim had revealed to a third classmate. Jim shot himself in the head using his parents' revolver on Monday morning, just as his parents were calling him to get ready for school" (Zinner, 1987, p. 499). Police came to the school later that morning to talk with Jim's teacher and a student whose name Jim had mentioned in a note he left. The classroom teacher notified other students at the school and their parents.

1. What memorial activities, if any, would you plan?

2. How will student attendance at the funeral be handled?

Consult "Responding to Suicide in Schools: A Case Study in Loss Intervention and Group Survivorship" (Zinner, 1987) for a detailed response plan.

A teacher collapses in the classroom. On February 13, 1992, a popular teacher at a Dallas-Fort Worth area high school collapsed in front of a classroom of students (Copilevitz, 1992). The school nurse was summoned and quickly began resuscitation efforts. Other staff who knew CPR came to help. Paramedics, who arrived a short time later, transported the teacher to the hospital where she was pronounced dead. Many students across the campus were deeply affected by the death of this teacher, who had taught math at the school for 6 years. A counseling team was called in to assist the students who had been in the classroom and others who were distraught after the death was announced.

1. What arrangements should the principal make the next day concerning a substitute for the classes this teacher taught?

2. What classroom activities may be helpful to students enrolled in this teacher's classes?

The murder of a junior high school principal traumatizes two campuses. The principal of a small, suburban junior high school was shot and killed by a 14-year-old student who had come to school that morning with "a semi-automatic rifle, a handgun, and pockets full of ammunition. The principal stepped out of his office, called him by name, and asked where he was going. When the shooting stopped, a student and two teachers lay wounded; [and] the principal . . . was dead" (Collison et al., 1987, p. 389). The student ran from the building, passed through an adjoining elementary school (in which the dead principal's son was a student), and into a nearby field. Television reporters arrived at the school as the principal was airlifted to a hospital and were present when police captured the student. Television stations played these graphic scenes repeatedly during the next week, further traumatizing students and parents in this small community.

1. What actions can school officials take to counteract the effects of the nightly newscasts?

2. What actions may be needed (at both the junior high and the elementary school) to assure parents and students that the schools are safe?

A death ignored leads to chaos. A popular 10th-grade student in a large, 5,000-student high school killed himself on a Wednesday. The school, which did not have a crisis plan, began organizing to respond to the death on Thursday. However, students did not attend school Friday because a severe hurricane hit the area. When school resumed Monday, "school officials assumed that, because things were quiet, the crisis was behind them. But on Wednesday a second student, the closest friend of the first suicide victim, took his life. The student body erupted with expressions of anger and outrage. . . ." (Phi Delta Kappa Task Force on Adolescent Suicide, 1988, p. 13).

1. What special actions may be needed to diffuse the anger and outrage students are exhibiting?

2. Devise a plan to be followed if another student suicide occurs.

A drowning death affects a school campus. On a Friday in late May, only a few days before school recessed for the summer, a 13-year-old boy drowned while fishing with a net in the shallow area of a local river. His twin brother and three other youths made desperate attempts to save the drowning youngster. Of the five boys, only one 12-year-old knew how to swim. The boys were all students at the same middle school.

1. Using the schema presented in chapter 2, determine the degree of trauma that can be expected campuswide.

2. Because school will recess for the summer in a few days, what special steps may be warranted?

A school bus accident kills three students. As he was driving to his office early one morning, the superintendent of a rural Virginia school district received a call about a school bus accident on a major highway. He drove immediately to the scene, where he found the bus on its side and many dazed, injured, and hysterical children. A large tractor-trailer truck had crashed into the rear of the bus as it stopped to pick up a waiting child. Emergency medical service personnel arrived and began treating the injured students. It was evident that there were fatalities, but emergency and school personnel could not determine the students' identities. Ambulances transported the injured students and the bus driver to area hospitals. The superintendent contacted the principals and asked that they notify the parents of children assigned to this bus.

The superintendent and principals, who met at the hospital where most of the children had been taken, determined that there had been three fatalities. Parents arriving at the hospitals in a state of panic found that the students who had died were at one hospital and the injured students at another. School personnel had identified all of the injured students and two of those who died. One of the deceased, a large girl, had severe injuries that made visual identification impossible. Because of the child's size, school personnel believed she was an upper-elementary school student, but the only child unaccounted for was a first grader. The dead student was finally identified when her mother described the clothes the child had worn that day. She was the missing first-grade student.

1. What types of counseling might the driver of this school bus, and perhaps other drivers in the district, need?

2. What actions will be needed to address the trauma of the students who were on this bus?

In September 1989, another tragic bus accident killed 21 students in a rural area of South Texas. As students were being transported to school one morning, their school bus fell into a water-filled pit after being rammed by a soft-drink delivery truck. Many students were trapped in the bus as it toppled over and became submerged in the water. As word of the accident spread, rescuers, including other students and family members, arrived and made desperate attempts to save the trapped students. In addition to the 21 deaths, 49 students were injured in this accident, some seriously. Many families in this small community were directly affected by these deaths, and students at the schools were grief-stricken. Every student knew someone who died in this tragedy.

1. Should schools be closed that day as word spreads about the accident? Why or why not?

2. What memorial activities might be appropriate in the following weeks in the schools and community?

A popular teacher's death requires immediate response. The principal was notified about midmorning on Thursday, just two days before the school would recess for spring break, that a teacher had died in her sleep. Miss Brown was a young, popular math teacher who sponsored the high school's dance team and pep squad. The 150 young women involved in these activities would be devastated by news of her death, and the impact on Miss Brown's math students and on the many young teachers at this school would be great. The principal knew that a well-planned response would need to be implemented quickly in this suburban high school of 2,000 students.

1. When and how should the death be announced to students and staff?

2. What actions will be needed that day and the next, considering that school will recess Friday afternoon for a week-long break?

Oates (1988) described in detail the actions taken in response to campuswide grief following this unexpected death.

The murders of two students in February 1992 were widely reported (Flax, 1992; Nordland, 1992). A 15-year-old student entered his high school in Brooklyn, walked up to two male students in a second-floor hallway, and shot them at close range in full view of many other students. The two students, a 16-year-old and a 17-year-old, died shortly afterward at a local hospital. The shootings occurred on a day when extra security guards were on duty because the mayor was coming to the campus. At the time of these deaths, "students were already mourning two other classmates who had been killed by firearms in the neighborhood over the previous weekend" (Flax, 1992, p. 22). Because 50 students in this school died violently in the past 5 years, the principal had established "grieving rooms" where students meet with campus and community counselors when a death occurs.

1. As a counselor in one of the grieving rooms, how will you help students process their grief?

2. As an administrator, what actions will you take regarding school safety in the future?

SUMMARY

Deaths that affect school campuses may involve students, teachers, and other staff members. These deaths may result from accidents, natural causes, or senseless violence. Some deaths cause considerable campuswide trauma, whereas others affect only a few students. How schools respond will depend on a number of factors including the degree of trauma, available staff and resources, location of the school, and community support. The responses in the four detailed case studies described above can serve as guides for school personnel who implement campus response plans. Each school community is different, however, and school personnel must develop a plan and take actions suited to their own special circumstances. Regardless of the actions taken, when calm returns after a crisis, the school's planning task force or key staff members should meet to consider the plans' effectiveness. Debriefing, an important but frequently slighted step in a comprehensive response plan, should not be omitted.

■ CONCLUSION ■

Responding to the Need

This book was written to assist those who must respond to the growing number of deaths, especially violent ones, that affect students, teachers, and staff in elementary and secondary schools nationwide. The statistics and examples in this publication dramatize the fact that tragic deaths occur in schools everywhere, small and large, and in rural areas and large cities alike. When a death affects a school community, there can be chaos or an orderly resolution of the trauma. The outcome depends largely on how effectively school staff respond, and effective responses require planning.

It is my hope that this book has encouraged school personnel to establish planning task forces, develop district and campus policies and procedures, and train staff members *before* their school is affected by a death. The detailed guides in this book can provide a starting point for those who develop a districtwide or campus plan, or for those who counsel with grieving students. The sample memoranda and forms can serve as models for announcing deaths, preparing for counseling groups, and notifying parents about actions taken. Ultimately, however, each campus and school district must assess carefully its own situation (i.e., location, available staff, resources, and community support) and tailor a plan to meet local needs.

The techniques and strategies for facilitating healthy grief responses as well as the counseling guides can give direction to those who work with grieving students. The detailed case studies illustrate how some schools assisted students when a death affected their school community. However, helping professionals must determine for themselves what techniques and formats would be appropriate and effective in their school and community. Developmental guidance programs stress the importance of offering grief support groups routinely, not only in the aftermath of a tragedy. Counselors and teachers who assist bereaved students (e.g.,those who experience the death of a parent or other close relative) throughout the school year are better prepared to respond when a tragic death affects a large number of students.

Although grief counseling for those who are bereaved is important, a developmental approach also calls for educational programs to help students learn about and acquire healthy attitudes toward death and dying. Unfortunately, only a few schools nationwide offer either death education or grief counseling programs. The reasons for the lack of programs are many, including the fact that we live in a death and grief denying society. Another reason is that teaching about death and assisting grieving students is usually the responsibility of teachers and counselors who often lack the training needed to perform these tasks. It is my belief that school counselors and teachers can be effective helpers, despite limited formal training in this field, if they understand grief reactions of school-age children and will work to resolve their own feelings about death. If this book has stimulated your interest in learning more about grief recovery, I encourage you to read books and journal articles or attend programs and workshops on this topic to increase your skills and knowledge. As you learn about grief recovery, you will realize that although intervening with a bereaved student may be uncomfortable for both you and the student, intervention is important.

Schonfeld and Kappelman (1992), who encouraged teachers not to shy away from discussing death with grieving students, observed:

> The child who is upset . . . is invariably expressing feelings and emotions that existed prior to the discussion; the teacher's willingness to "hear" these feelings is the reason that the child is able to express them. The discussion did not cause the upset, but only allowed its expression, a needed first step toward its resolution. (p. 27)

Grief therapist Alan Wolfelt (1983) also suggested that teachers and counselors should not avoid "what a grieving child is feeling because we are afraid he/she cannot take it. Obviously the child is already taking it. The question is 'Will the child experience these feelings in isolation or in the comfort of loving adults?' " (p. 72).

Some educators may believe that providing assistance to grieving students is beyond the scope of their responsibility. Others fail to act because they believe they are not qualified. Whatever reasons we pose for not helping, the fact remains that students do not leave their grief at the schoolhouse door. It is my hope that educators, whose business *is* education, will be eager to learn more about children's grief in order to plan and implement helpful responses. Counselors and teachers who acknowledge and normalize bereaved children's feelings; address their fears and fantasies; offer emotional support; and assist them in commemorating the life of the person who died provide a valuable service not only to bereaved students but also to the school as a whole. If schools respond effectively, students and staff will more than survive—they will learn and grow from a death that affects the school community.

References

About grief, a scriptographic booklet. (1990). South Deerfield, MA: Channing L. Bete.

Adler, C. S., Stanford, G., & Adler, S. M. (Eds.). (1976). *We are but a moment's sunlight, understanding death.* New York: Pocket Books.

Allan, J., & Anderson, E. (1986). Children and crises: A classroom guidance approach. *Elementary School Guidance & Counseling, 21*, 143–149.

Alexander, J. A. C., & Harman, R. R. (1988). One counselor's intervention in the aftermath of a middle school student's suicide: A case study. *Journal of Counseling and Development, 66*, 283–285.

Arena, C., Hermann, J., & Hoffman, T. (1984). Helping children deal with the death of a classmate: A crisis intervention model. *Elementary School Guidance & Counseling, 19*, 107–115.

Atkinson, T. C. (1980). Teacher intervention with elementary school children in death related situations. *Death Education, 4*, 149–163.

At-risk youth in crisis: A handbook for collaboration between schools and social services. (1991). [Volume 2: Suicide]. Eugene, OR: Linn-Benton Education Service Center and ERIC Clearinghouse on Educational Management.

Barrett, T. C. (1989). *Teens in crisis.* Arlington, VA: American Association of School Administrators.

Baxter, G. (1982). Bereavement support groups for secondary school students. *School Guidance Worker, 38*, 27–29.

Bernardt, G. R., & Praeger, S. G. (1985). Preventing child suicide: The elementary school death education puppet show. *Journal of Counseling and Development, 63*, 311–312.

Bernstein, J. E. (1989). *Books to help children cope with separation and loss: An annotated bibliography* (3rd ed.). New York: Bowker.

Bertoia, J., & Allan, J. (1988). School management of the bereaved child. *Elementary School Guidance & Counseling, 23*, 30–37.

Bodinger-deUriarte, C. (1991, December). *Hate crime: The rise of hate crime on school campuses* [Research Bulletin, No. 10]. Bloomington, IN: Phi Delta Kappa, Center for Evaluation, Development, and Research.

Bowlby, J. (1979). *The making and breaking of affectional bonds.* London: Tavistock.

Brown, S. L. (1991). *Counseling victims of violence.* Alexandria, VA: American Association for Counseling and Development.

Capuzzi, D., & Golden, L. (1988). *Preventing adolescent suicide.* Muncie, IN: Accelerated Development.

Carroll, M. R. (1977). About this issue. *The School Counselor, 24,* 307.

Carter S. R. (1987). Use of puppets to treat traumatic grief: A case study. *Elementary School Guidance & Counseling, 21,* 210–215.

Center for the Study of Social Policy. (1991). *Kids count data book, state profiles of child well-being.* Washington, DC: Author. (Eric document no. 328–553).

Center to Prevent Handgun Violence. (1990, September). *Caught in the crossfire: A report on gun violence in our nation's schools.* Washington, DC: Author.

Centers for Disease Control. (1988, August 19). CDC recommendations for a community plan for the prevention and containment of suicide clusters. *Morbidity and Mortality, Weekly Report (MMWR), 37,* 1–12. Atlanta, GA: U.S. Department of Health and Human Services, Public Health Service.

Centers for Disease Control. (1991, March 22). Alcohol-related traffic fatalities among youth and young adults—United States, 1982–89. *MMWR, 40,* 178–179, 185. Atlanta, GA: U.S. Department of Health and Human Services, Public Health Service.

Centers for Disease Control. (1991, May 24). Adolescent suicide and suicide attempts—Santa Fe County, New Mexico, January 1985–May 1990. *MMWR, 40,* 329–331. Atlanta, GA: U.S. Department of Health and Human Services, Public Health Service.

Centers for Disease Control. (1991, September 20). Attempted suicide among high school students—United States, 1990. *MMWR, 40,* 633–636. Atlanta, GA: U.S. Department of Health and Human Services, Public Health Service.

Centers for Disease Control. (1991, October 11). Weapon-carrying among high school students—United States, 1990. *MMWR, 40,* 681–684. Atlanta, GA: U.S. Department of Health and Human Services, Public Health Service.

Colgrove, M., Bloomfield, H., & McWilliams, P. (1976). *How to survive the loss of a love.* New York: Bantam Books.

Collison, B., Bowden, S., Patterson, M., Snyder, J., Sandall, S., & Wellman, P. (1987). After the shooting stops. *Journal of Counseling and Development, 65,* 389–390.

Copilevitz, T. (1992, February 14). Teacher dies after collapsing in classroom. *The Dallas Morning News,* pp. 25A, 28A.

Corr, C. A. (1984). Helping with death education. In H. Wass & C. A. Corr (Eds.), *Helping children cope with death: Guidelines and resources* (2nd ed., pp. 49–73). Washington, DC: Hemisphere.

Crenshaw, D. A. (1990). *Bereavement.* New York: Continuum.

Danto, B. L. (1978). Crisis intervention in a classroom regarding the homicide of a teacher. *The School Counselor, 26,* 69–89.

Doherty, S. (1989, November 13). Teaching kids how to grieve. *Newsweek,* p. 73.

Doka, K. J. (1989). *Disenfranchised grief: Recognizing hidden sorrow.* Lexington, MA: Lexington Books.

Dunne-Maxim, K., Dunne, E. J., & Hauser, M. J. (1987). When children are suicide survivors. In E. J. Dunne, J. L. McIntosh, & K. Dunne-Maxim (Eds.), *Suicide and its aftermath* (pp. 234–244). New York: Norton.

Edwards, T. (1990, May 14). Teen who died in fire feared life in jeopardy, friend says. *San Antonio Express-News,* p. 11A.

Edwards, T. (1992, February 17). Gang crashes party; Girl killed, 8 injured. *San Antonio Express-News,* p. 1A, 4A.

Egge, D. L., Marks, L. G., & McEvers, D. M. (1987). Puppets and adolescents: A group guidance workshop approach. *Elementary School Guidance & Counseling, 21,* 183–192.

Eisenberg, L. (1986). Does bad news about suicide beget bad news? *New England Journal of Medicine, 315,* 705–707.

Eth, S., & Pynoos, R. S. (Eds.). (1985). *Post-traumatic stress disorder in children.* Washington, DC: American Psychiatric.

Flax, E. (1992, March 25). Coping in the middle of a war zone at Jefferson High. *Education Week,* pp. 1, 22.

Freeman, J. (1978). Death and dying in three days? *Phi Delta Kappan, 60,*118.

Freeman, S. J. (1991). Group facilitation of the grieving process with those bereaved by suicide. *Journal of Counseling & Development, 69,* 328–331.

Furman, E. (1984). Children's patterns in mourning the death of a loved one. In H. Wass & C. A. Corr (Eds.), *Childhood and death* (pp. 185–203). Washington, DC: Hemisphere.

Gang members charged in slaying of boy, 14. (1991, December 28). *San Antonio Express-News,* p. 2B.

Gladding, S. T. (1992). *Counseling as an art:The creative arts in counseling.* Alexandria, VA: American Association for Counseling and Development.

Gladding, S. T., & Gladding, C. (1991). The abcs of bibliotherapy for school counselors. *The School Counselor, 39,* 7–13.

Glass, J. C. (1991). Death, loss, and grief among middle school children: Implications for the school counselor. *Elementary School Guidance & Counseling, 26,* 139–148.

Gordon, A. K., & Klass, D. (1979). *They need to know: How to teach children about death.* Englewood Cliffs, NJ: Prentice-Hall.

Gray, R. E. (1988). The role of school counselors with bereaved teenagers: With and without peer support groups. *The School Counselor, 35,* 185–193.

Griggs, S. A. (1977). Annotated bibliography of books on death, dying, and bereavement. *The School Counselor, 24,* 362–371.

Grollman, E. A. (1990). *Talking about death: A dialogue between parent and child* (3rd ed.). Boston: Beacon Press.

Haasl, B., & Marnocha, J. (1990). *Bereavement support group program for children*. Muncie, IN: Accelerated Development.

Herring, R. (1990). Suicide in the middle school: Who said kids will not? *Elementary School Guidance & Counseling, 25*, 129–137.

Hiratsuka, J. (1989, April). School shooting evokes a crisis response. *NASW NEWS*, p. 9.

Holmes, T. H., & Rahe, R. H. (1967). The social readjustment rating scale. *Journal of Psychosomatic Research, 11*, 213–218.

Hopson, J. L. (1988). A pleasurable chemistry. *Psychology Today, 22* (7), 29–33.

Hunt, C. (1987). Step by step: How your school can live through the tragedy of teen suicides. *The American School Board Journal, 174*, 34–37.

It's not just New York . . . . (1992, March 9). *Newsweek*, pp. 25–26, 29.

James, J. W., & Cherry, F. (1988). *The grief recovery handbook: A step-by-step program for moving beyond loss*. New York: Harper & Row.

Janosik, E. H. (1986). *Crisis counseling: A contemporary approach*. Boston: Jones & Bartlett.

Jewett, C. L. (1982). *Helping children cope with separation and loss*. Harvard, MA: The Harvard Common Press.

Johnson, S. W., & Maile, L. J. (1987). *Suicide and the schools*. Springfield, IL: Charles C Thomas.

Jones, W. H. (1977). Death-related grief counseling: The school counselor's responsibility. *The School Counselor, 24*, 315–320.

Jozefowski, J. (1983). Children's concepts of death. In D. M. Moriarty (Ed.), *The loss of loved ones* (pp. 250–282). St. Louis: Warren H. Green.

Jukes, M. (1985). *Blackberries in the dark*. New York: Yearling.

Kalish, R. A., & Reynolds, D. K. (1981). *Death and ethnicity: A psychocultural study*. Farmingdale, NY: Baywood.

Knowles, D. W., & Reeves, N. (1983). *Won't Granny need her socks?* Dubuque, IA: Kendall/Hunt.

Kolehmainen, J., & Handwerk, S. (1986). *Teen suicide, A book for friends, family and classmates*. Minneapolis: Lerner.

Kopp, R. (1983). *Where has Grandpa gone? Helping children cope with grief and loss*. Grand Rapids, MI: Zondervan.

Kübler-Ross, E. (1969). *On death and dying*. New York: Macmillan.

Landers, A. (1983). Counseling works. *Chicago Tribune*.

Lane, E. (1991, September 24). Teacher killed in store robbery. *San Antonio Express-News*, pp. 1A, 4A.

Lawton, M. (1991, November 6). Why are children turning to guns? *Education Week*, pp. 1, 14–15.

Lieberman, M., & Borman, L. (1979). *Self-help groups for coping with crises*. San Francisco: Jossey-Bass.

Lobel, B., & Hirschfeld, R. (1984). *Depression: What we know.* [DHHS Publication No. (ADM) 85–1318]. Rockville, MD: U.S. Department of Health and Human Services, National Institute of Mental Health.

Lonetto, R., & Templer, D. I. (1986). *Death anxiety.* Washington, DC: Hemisphere.

Love, P. (1991). *The emotional incest syndrome: What to do when a parent's love rules your life.* New York: Bantam Books.

Magno, J. (1990). The hospice concept of care: Facing the 1990s. *Death Studies, 14,* 109–119.

Markusen, E., & Fulton, R. (1971). Childhood bereavement and behavior disorders: A critical review. *Omega, 2,* 107–117.

McComb, B. (1978). Children require reality. *The School Counselor, 26,* 95.

Modrak, R. (1992, January). Mass shootings and airplane crashes: Counselors respond to the changing face of community crisis. *Guidepost,* p. 4.

Moore, T. E., & Mae, R. (1987). Who dies and who cries: Death and bereavement in children's literature. *Journal of Communication, 37,* 52–64.

Moriarty, D. M. (Ed.). (1983). *The loss of loved ones: The effects of a death in the family on personality development.* St. Louis: Warren H. Green.

Mueller, J. M. (1978). I taught about death and dying. *Phi Delta Kappan, 60,* 117.

National Association of Secondary School Principals. (1986, December). *How to handle death in the school: Tips for principals from NASSP.* Reston, VA: Author.

National Center for Health Statistics [NCHS]. (1992, January 7). Report for final mortality statistics, 1989. *Monthly Vital Statistics Report* [Supplement 2], *40*(8). Atlanta, GA: U.S. Department of Health and Human Services, Public Health Service.

Nordland, R. (1992, March 9). Deadly lessons. *Newsweek,* pp. 22–24.

Oaklander, V. (1988). *Windows to our children.* Highland, NY: The Center for Gestalt Development.

Oates, M. (1988). Responding to death in the schools. *TACD Journal, 16,* 83–96.

Office of Educational Research and Improvement (OERI), U.S. Department of Education. (1991). *Youth indicators 1991: Trends in the well-being of American youth.* Washington, DC: Author.

Palmo, A. J., Langlois, D. E., & Bender, I. (1988). Development of a policy and procedures statement for crisis situations in the school. *The School Counselor, 36,* 94–102.

Pelej, J. (1987, April). Help your school survive a suicide. *The Executive Educator, 26*–31.

Petersen, S., & Straub, R. L. (1992). *School crisis survival guide.* West Nyack, NY: The Center for Applied Research in Education.

Pfeifer, J. K. (1986). *Teenage suicide: What can the schools do?* [PDK Fastback No. 234]. Bloomington, IN: Phi Delta Kappa Educational Foundation.

Phi Delta Kappa Task Force on Adolescent Suicide. (1988). *Responding to adolescent suicide.* Bloomington, IN: Phi Delta Kappa Educational Foundation.

Powers, T. (1971, June). Learning to die. *Harper's Magazine,* pp. 72–80.

Raymer, M., & McIntyre, B. B. (1987). *The art of grief.* Traverse City, MI: Grand Traverse Area Hospice.

Reading, writing—and violence. (1991, November 24). *The Orlando Sentinel, Florida Edition,* pp. A1, A14.

Redmond, L. M. (1989). *Surviving: When someone you love was murdered.* Clearwater, FL: Psychological Consultation and Educational Services.

Schaefer, D., & Lyons, C. (1988). *How do we tell the children? Helping children understand and cope when someone dies.* New York: Newmarket.

Schonfeld, D., & Kappelman, M. (1992, March 4). Teaching the toughest lesson—about death. *Education Week,* pp. 25, 27.

Schools add to curriculum after suicides. (1992, January 26). *The Dallas Morning News,* p. 36A.

Siehl, P. M. (1990). Suicide postvention: A new disaster plan—what a school should do when faced with a suicide. *The School Counselor, 38,* 52–57.

Sklar, F., & Hartley, S. F. (1990). Close friends as survivors: Bereavement patterns in a "hidden" population. *Omega, 21,* 103–112.

Slaikeu, K. A. (1990). *Crisis intervention: A handbook for practice and research* (2nd ed.). Boston: Allyn & Bacon.

Smith, A. C., & Borgers, S. B. (1988–89). Parental grief response to perinatal death. *Omega, 19,* 203–212.

Sommerfeld, M. (1992a, May 13). Classes to resume at California school where gunman killed 4 and wounded 9. *Education Week,* p. 4.

Sommerfeld, M. (1992b, May 20). Informal network brings welcome help to officials coping with school traumas. *Education Week,* p. 4.

Stanford, G. (1977a). Introduction. *The School Counselor, 24,* 308–309.

Stanford, G. (1977b). Methods and materials for death education. *The School Counselor, 24,* 350–360.

Stefanowski-Harding, S. (1990). Child suicide: A review of the literature and implications for school counselors. *The School Counselor, 37,* 328–336.

Students mourning 3 teen-age suicides. (1990, May 3). *San Antonio Express-News,* p. 12A.

Tatelbaum, J. (1980). *The courage to grieve.* New York: Harper & Row.

U.S. Bureau of the Census. (1991). *Statistical abstract of the United States: 1991* (111th ed.). Washington, DC: Author.

Van Dexter, J. D. (1986). Anticipatory grief: Strategies for the classroom. In T. A. Rando (Ed.), *Loss and anticipatory grief* (pp. 155–173). Lexington, MA: Lexington Books.

Vinturella, L., & James, R. (1987). Sandplay: A therapeutic medium with children. *Elementary School Guidance & Counseling, 21,* 229–238.

Ward, P. (1991, December 15). Violence invades young lives. *The* (Austin, TX) *American-Statesman,* pp. A1, A28.

Wass, H. (1984a). Concepts of death: A developmental perspective. In H. Wass & C. A. Corr (Eds.), *Childhood and death* (pp. 3–24). Washington, DC: Hemisphere.

Wass, H. (1984b). Parents, teachers, and health professionals as helpers. In H. Wass & C. A. Corr (Eds.), *Helping children cope with death: Guidelines and resources* (2nd ed., pp. 75–130). Washington, DC: Hemisphere.

Wass, H., & Corr, C. A. (Eds.). (1984a). *Childhood and death.* Washington, DC: Hemisphere.

Wass, H., & Corr, C. A. (Eds.). (1984b). *Helping children cope with death: Guidelines and resources.* Washington, DC: Hemisphere.

Wass, H., Miller, M. D., & Thornton, G. (1990). Death education and grief/suicide interventions in the public schools. *Death Studies, 14,* 253–268.

Wass, H., Raup, J., & Sisler, H. (1989). Adolescents and death on television: A follow up study. *Death Studies, 13,* 161–173.

Watson, R. S., Poda, J. H., Miller C. T., Rice, E. S., & West, G. (1990). *Containing crisis: A guide to managing school emergencies.* Bloomington, IN: National Educational Service.

Wolfelt, A. (1983). *Helping children cope with grief.* Muncie, IN: Accelerated Development.

Yalom, I. D. (1985). *The theory & practice of group psychotherapy.* New York: Basic Books.

Zinner, E. S. (1985). Group survivorship: A model and case application. In E. S. Zinner (Ed.), *Coping with death on campus* (pp. 51–68). San Francisco: Jossey-Bass.

Zinner, E. S. (1987). Responding to suicide in schools: A case study in loss intervention and group survivorship. *Journal of Counseling and Development, 65,* 499–501.

Zinner, E. S. (1990). Survivors of suicide: Understanding and coping with the legacy of self-inflicted death. In P. Cimbolic & D. A. Jobes (Eds.), *Youth suicide: Issues, assessment, and intervention* (pp. 67–85). Springfield, IL: Charles C Thomas.

■ APPENDIX A ■

Annotated Bibliography
and Resources

LOSS AND GRIEF THEORY AND
HELPING STRATEGIES

Books

Adler, C. S., Stanford, G., & Adler, S. M. (Eds.). (1976). *We are but a moment's sunlight, understanding death.* New York: Pocket Books.
A book of essays and other genre from the world's best literature for adults and older students who want to confront their beliefs, attitudes, and fears about death. Topics include perceptions of death, the process of dying, what comes after death, customs for coping with death, grief and mourning, and suicide.

Colgrove, M., Bloomfield, H., & McWilliams, P. (1991). *How to survive the loss of a love.* Los Angeles: Prelude.
This brief book of thoughts, poems, and affirmations provides comfort to those suffering a loss. Although written about the loss of a romantic love partner, the practical suggestions for emotional survival are applicable to any loss. Information in this book will be useful to leaders and members of loss and grief support groups.

Crenshaw, D. A. (1990). *Bereavement.* New York: Continuum.
Written for a general audience as well as professionals, this book presents information about grieving children and adults at different developmental stages. The author discusses reactions to different deaths (e.g., that of siblings, classmates, or parents), coping strategies, and counseling needs of preschoolers, school-age children, adolescents, and adults.

DeSpelder, L., & Strickland, A. (1983). *The last dance: Encountering death and dying.* Palo Alto: Mayfield.
Written as a textbook for college-level death education courses, this book will be helpful to educators who have not studied death and dying. Provides infor-

mation about the historical, sociological, and theoretical bases of almost every aspect of the subject.

Donnelly, N. H. (1987). *I never know what to say: How to help your family and friends cope with tragedy*. New York: Ballantine.

Written by a hospital chaplain based on her personal experience with death and with relatives and friends of dying and deceased children. It describes well the grieving process children and teenagers experience and gives concrete suggestions of what to do and say to the bereaved.

Dunne, E. J., McIntosh, J. L., & Dunne-Maxim, K. (Eds.). (1987). *Suicide and its aftermath*. New York: Norton.

A scholarly publication focusing on the needs of those who survive a loved one's suicide. Several chapters—"When Children are Suicide Survivors," "Special Aspects of Grief After a Suicide," "Self-Help and Support Groups," and "Postvention in Schools: Policy and Process"—will interest educators.

James, J. W., & Cherry, F. (1988). *The grief recovery handbook: A step-by-step program for moving beyond loss*. New York: Harper & Row.

Written by the cofounders of the Grief Recovery Institute, this book can assist counselors and teachers who want to help grieving students, but first need to recover from a loss they themselves have experienced.

Jewett, C. L. (1982). *Helping children cope with separation and loss*. Harvard, MA: The Harvard Common Press.

Provides detailed information about the grief recovery process in young children and strategies for helping at each stage. In addition to death, the author addresses losses related to parents' divorce or separation and entering or leaving foster care.

Klagsbrun, F. (1985). *Too young to die: Youth and suicide*. New York: Pocket Books.

Updated periodically, this paperback addresses the scope of the problem, the warning signs of suicide, how suicide affects survivors, and how our culture views suicide.

Kolehmainen, J., & Handwerk, S. (1986). *Teen suicide, a book for friends, family, and classmates*. Minneapolis: Lerner.

An easy-to-read book for survivors and those who may know a potentially suicidal teen. The authors use fictionalized vignettes from the lives of hurting teens to illustrate the facts and myths of suicide.

Kopp, R. (1983). *Where has grandpa gone? Helping children cope with grief and loss.* Grand Rapids, MI: Zondervan.

Written for parents and educators, this book provides examples of how to explain death (with a Christian emphasis) to children. Describes children's reactions to losses other than death and has a "read-aloud" section that can be used to answer young children's questions.

Kübler-Ross, E. (1982). *Working it through, an Elizabeth Kübler-Ross workshop on life, death and transition.* New York: Macmillan.

Describes Kübler-Ross's workshops with terminally ill individuals, those grieving a death, and professionals who work with death and dying.

Kushner, H. S. (1981). *When bad things happen to good people.* New York: Schocken.

Rabbi Kushner wrote this book (following his son's death from a rare and painful disease) for people who "want to believe in God's goodness and fairness," but find believing difficult when they are "hurt by life—by death, illness or injury, rejection or disappointment." It is a thought-provoking book that provides knowledge useful to those who assist the bereaved.

Schaefer, D., & Lyons, C. (1988). *How do we tell the children? Helping children understand and cope when someone dies.* New York: Newmarket.

Discusses children's understanding of and reactions to death at different ages. Provides scripts for explaining death from many causes including suicide, homicide, and old age. An excellent resource for parents, teachers, and counselors who work with very young children, and teachers of high school child development courses.

Tatelbaum, J. (1980). *The courage to grieve.* New York: Harper & Row.

Provides information for professional and nonprofessional readers on the theory of grief recovery and helping strategies. This book can be helpful to educators who need to resolve their own grief or learn about the grief process to be effective helpers. It is also useful for those who lead support groups and as assigned reading for group members.

Wass, H., & Corr, C. A. (Eds.). (1984). *Childhood and death.* Washington, DC: Hemisphere.

A comprehensive, scholarly collection of information about death, dying, bereavement, and death education. Of special interest to educators are selections on "Helping Siblings and Other Peers Cope With Dying," "Teachable Moments Occasioned by 'Small Deaths' " (about death education and grief support with elementary children), and "Death Education in the Schools for Older Children." A selected resource guide with books for adults and children is included.

Wass, H., & Corr, C. A. (Eds.). (1984). *Helping children cope with death: Guidelines and resources* (2nd ed.). Washington, DC: Hemisphere.

Discusses basic requirements for being helpers and describes research and clinical findings about children and death. An annotated bibliography of 44 books for adults, 160 books for children, and 154 audiovisual resources is included.

Wolfelt, A. (1983). *Helping children cope with grief.* Muncie: IN: Accelerated Development.

This book, written by an experienced grief therapist, gives educators and parents information about children's reactions to death. Almost one third of the book is devoted to developing the skills needed to assist grieving children. A list of books and other resources for grieving children and those who work with them is included.

Journal Articles

Alexander, J. A., & Harman, R. R. (1988). One counselor's intervention in the aftermath of a middle school student's suicide: A case study. *Journal of Counseling and Development, 66,* 283–285.

A middle school counselor meets the needs of grieving classmates after a 13-year-old kills himself. Describes classroom visits and small group counseling sessions in which the counselor uses Gestalt techniques.

Danto, B. L. (1978). Crisis intervention in a classroom regarding the homicide of a teacher. *The School Counselor, 26,* 69–89.

Describes school and community responses to the death of a teacher who was murdered in front of her second-grade class. Articles by professionals responding to Danto's account are included in this special edition of *The School Counselor.*

Freeman, S. J. (1991). Group facilitation of the grieving process with those bereaved by suicide. *Journal of Counseling & Development, 69,* 328–331.

Describes an eight-session counseling group for suicide survivors. Discusses the theory upon which strategies and activities are based. Although the group was designed for adults meeting in a community center, some techniques used are appropriate for school counseling groups.

Lagrand, L. E. (1991). United we cope: Support groups for the dying and bereaved. *Death Studies, 15,* 2^7–230.

Discusses the development of the self-help movement, with special attention to the effectiveness of support groups for the bereaved. Analyzes two groups—

the Compassionate Friends (for bereaved parents) and Make Today Count (for cancer patients and their families).

Moore, T. E., & Mae, R. (1987). Who dies and who cries: Death and bereavement in children's literature. *Journal of Communication, 37*, 52–64.

The authors analyzed children's books published between 1970 and 1983 to determine the primary character, the type of death, and the effect of the death on the primary character. They found that many books do not portray the grief process accurately.

The School Counselor, 24(5) [Special Issue on Death] (1977).

This special issue focuses on school counselors' role in assisting grieving students, serving as consultants to teachers, and developing death education programs. Although the articles were written more than 10 years ago, much of the material is still timely and relevant.

Smith, I. (1991). Preschool children "play" out their grief. *Death Studies, 15*, 169–176.

This article describes grief reactions of very young children and helping strategies used with those who come to a special community program at the Dougy Center located in Portland, Oregon.

Vickio, C. J. (1990). The goodbye brochure: Helping students to cope with transition or loss. *Journal of Counseling & Development, 68*, 575–577.

Describes a brochure designed for college students that includes the "five D's for successfully dealing with departure and loss." The information can be adapted for use with middle and high school students.

Vinturella, L., & James, R. (1987). Sandplay: A therapeutic medium with children. *Elementary School Guidance & Counseling, 21*, 229–238.

Discusses sand play, a form of play therapy useful for diagnostic and therapeutic purposes. Describes six counseling sessions using a sand table with an 8-year-old boy following the death of his father.

Zinner, E. S. (1987). Responding to suicide in schools: A case study in loss intervention and group survivorship. *Journal of Counseling and Development, 65*, 499-501.

Describes in detail an excellent plan of action following the suicide of a sixth-grade student in a small, private school. Counseling strategies helped students remember the life and the death of the deceased, prepare to attend the funeral, and plan group rituals.

CRISIS MANAGEMENT PLANNING

At-risk youth in crisis: A handbook for collaboration between schools and social services [Volume 2: Suicide]. (1991). Eugene, OR: Linn-Benton Education Service District/ERIC Clearinghouse on Educational Management.

A handbook that promotes school and community agency cooperation and shared responsibility in suicide prevention and response after a death. Discusses policy and procedure development, including legal requirements and ramifications of school response. Provides examples of crisis management plans.

Collison, B., et al. (1987). After the shooting stops. *Journal of Counseling and Development, 65,* 389–390.

Describes how two schools responded following the death of a junior high school principal shot by a student who escaped through a nearby elementary school. The author discusses candidly strategies that worked in this difficult situation as well as things the staff wishes they had done differently.

Johnson, S. W., & Maile, L. J. (1987). *Suicide and the schools.* Springfield, IL: Charles C Thomas.

Discusses prevention, intervention, postvention, characteristics of at-risk students, and the roles and responsibilities of school personnel. Provides outlines for suicide prevention workshops used with parents and students.

Kelly, D. G. (1991). Anatomy of a tragedy. *The School Administrator, 48* (5), 8–11.

A school superintendent critiques one district's response to campus-wide trauma following the death of a teacher whose body was found hanging in his classroom.

National Association of Secondary School Principals. (December, 1987). Student stress and suicide. *The Practitioner, 14* (2). Reston, VA: Author.

This edition of a "newsletter for the on-line administrator" discusses suicide prevention, intervention, and postvention strategies. It gives case examples from school districts across the United States that emphasize community participation in planning prevention measures.

Palmo, A. J., Langlois, D., & Bender, I. (1988). Development of a policy and procedures statement for crisis situations in the school. *The School Counselor, 36,* 94–102.

Discusses legal implications of providing for students in crisis (with case examples) and the need to create awareness within the school and community.

Suggests guidelines administrators should consider when establishing crisis policy and procedures.

Petersen, S., & Straub, R. L. (1992). *School crisis survival guide.* West Nyack, NY: The Center for Applied Research in Education.

Provides practical ideas for responding to crises that affect schools, such as deaths and natural disasters. Topics include establishing districtwide and campus crisis teams, interfacing with the media, and counseling grieving or traumatized students.

Phi Delta Kappa Task Force on Adolescent Suicide. (1988). *Responding to adolescent suicide.* Bloomington, IN: Phi Delta Kappa Educational Foundation.

An excellent, 29-page booklet about prevention, postvention, and intervention measures. Provides a 10-step action plan for use following a suicide and guidelines for districtwide and campus-based crisis teams.

Watson, R. S., Poda, J. H., Miller C. T., Rice, E. S., & West, G. (1990). *Containing crisis: A guide to managing school emergencies.* Bloomington, IN: National Educational Service.

Written by educators experienced in responding to serious school emergencies, this book provides detailed information of special interest to administrators. Topics covered include dealing with rumors, managing parent reactions, and staff training. Sample districtwide and campus emergency response plans are included.

BOOKS FOR CHILDREN AND ADOLESCENTS

Agee, J. (1969). *A death in the family.* New York: Bantam.

A Pulitzer Prize-winning novel appropriate for use with high school students. Provides insight into how death affects a family, including the misunderstandings that often occur.

Bunting, E. (1982). *The happy funeral.* New York: Harper & Row.

A young Chinese girl grieves the death of her grandfather. She helps prepare for his funeral and is comforted by cultural rituals. Suitable for ages 6 to 13.

Clardy, A. F. (1984). *Dusty was my friend.* New York: Human Sciences.

A young boy tells about the death of his friend killed in an automobile accident. This book shows how sharing memories of the deceased alleviates the pain of grieving. Appropriate for ages 5 to 12.

Cohen, B. (1974). *Thank you, Jackie Robinson.* New York: Lothrop.

Sam, aged 12, becomes acquainted with Davy, a 60-year-old Black man through their mutual love of baseball and Jackie Robinson. Sam's father had been dead for 5 years when he met Davy, who becomes both a father-figure and friend. When Davy dies of a heart attack, Sam mourns deeply, but is resilient.

Cohen, J. (1987). *I had a friend named Peter.* New York: Morrow.

Written by an experienced counselor, this illustrated book can help children ages 6 through 12 who are grieving the death of a peer. The story is about a young girl, Betsy, who is troubled and has many questions when her best friend dies.

Fassler, J. (1971). *My grandpa died today.* New York: Human Sciences.

An ailing grandfather tries to prepare his grandson, David, for his death. Although his grandfather's death saddens him greatly, David is able to resume his usual pursuits rather quickly (a normal reaction for a child his age). Well illustrated and appropriate for ages 5 to 8.

Greene, C. C. (1976). *Beat the turtle drum.* New York: Viking.

After her younger sister dies (at age 11) when she falls from a tree, a young girl experiences emotions common after a sibling death—loneliness, anger, confusion over her parents' reactions, and deep sadness. Useful for parents, educators, and upper elementary students.

Gunther, J. (1971). *Death be not proud.* New York: Harper & Row.

Chronicles a courageous teenager's decline and death from a brain tumor. A nonfiction book for middle and high school students.

Hammond, J. (1981). *When my daddy died and when my mommy died.* Cincinnati: Cranbrook.

A book of simple drawings and text for young children ages 4 and up.

Huntsberry, W. E. (1970). *The big hangup.* New York: Lothrop.

Teenagers deal with their grief and guilt after a friend dies in an automobile accident involving teenage drinking and driving. Starkly realistic, this story shows the guilt and self-blame that many teens feel after a tragic accident.

Kolehmainen, J., & Handwerk, S. (1986). *Teen suicide, a book for friends, family, and classmates.* Minneapolis: Lerner.

An easy-to-read book for survivors and those who may know a potentially suicidal teen. The authors use fictionalized vignettes from the lives of hurting teens to illustrate the facts and myths of suicide.

LeShan, E. (1988). *Learning to say goodbye: When a parent dies.* New York: Avon.

A book for children ages 8 and older, but also helpful to adults who need to understand how loss affects children. Describes common feelings after the death of a parent and how to work through one's grief.

Miles, M. (1971). *Annie and the Old One.* Boston: Little, Brown.

This classic, fictional story of an Indian grandmother's explanation of death to a young child is appropriate for children ages 6 to 11. The grandmother believes that she will die when she finishes the rug she is weaving. Teaches that death is a natural part of the life cycle.

Richter, E. (1986). *Losing someone you love: When a brother or sister dies.* New York: Putnam.

Young people ages 10 to 24 discuss candidly their experiences following the death of a sibling.

Rofes, E. (Ed.). (1985). *Kid's book about death and dying.* Boston: Little, Brown.

Students, ages 11 to 14, explore their feelings and thoughts about death and grief ranging from causes of death, euthanasia, and funerals to graveyards. Suitable for ages 10 to 17.

Stein, S. B. (1984). *About dying: An open family book for children and parents together.* New York: Walker.

An illustrated book that parents or teachers can use to explain death as part of the life cycle to young children. Information is included for the adult to read before using the book with children ages 3 to 9.

Zindel, P. (1976). *Pardon me, you're stepping on my eyeball* and *The pigman.* (1968). New York: Harper.

The true-to-life situations in these two books about teenagers living in less-than-ideal families appeal to young people. Death is a recurring theme, especially in *The Pigman.*

Zolotow, C. (1974). *My grandson Lew.* New York: Harper.

A 6-year-old boy and his mother share their memories of the boy's beloved grandfather. Because Lewis was only 2 when the grandfather died, his mother had not discussed the death with him. The child's memories comfort his mother in her grief. Appropriate for children ages 5 or older as well as adults.

OTHER RESOURCES

Publications

Bernstein, J. E. (1989). *Books to help children cope with separation and loss (3rd ed.)*. New York: Bowker.

An excellent annotated bibliography of books children can read to help them through their grief. There are sections for different types of loss including adoption, moving, divorce, and death. The interest level and readling level is given for more than 400 entries. The use of bibliotherapy is discussed.

Death Studies, edited by Robert A. Neimeyer, Department of Psychology, Memphis State University, Memphis TN.

A professional journal published bimonthly by Hemisphere Publishing Corporation, 79 Madison Avenue, Suite 1110, New York, NY 10016. Articles address many different aspects of death and dying.

The *Good Grief Program* offers counseling to children in the Boston area and provides resource materials for counselors. For information contact the Good Grief Program, Judge Baker Children's Center, 295 Longwood Avenue, Boston, MA 02115. Telephone: 617/232-8390.

Haasl, B. S., & Marnocha, J. (1990). *Bereavement support group program for children*. Muncie, IN: Accelerated Development.

The authors established a grief support group for children ages 5 to 15 in a community agency. A leader's guide and participant workbooks for use in a five-session group are available from the publisher. The materials are most appropriate for use with children ages 5 to 11.

Omega, edited by Robert J. Kastenbaum, Gerontology and Aging Studies, Arizona State University, Tempe, AZ 85281.

An international professional journal published quarterly by Baywood Publishing Company, P. O. Box 337, Amityville, NY 11701. Articles focus on the study of death and dying.

Pfeifer, J. K. (1986). *Teenage suicide: What can the schools do?* [PDK Fastback No. 234]. Bloomington, IN: Phi Delta Kappa Educational Foundation.

This brief booklet is excellent for sensitizing teachers and staff to the problem of suicide among secondary school students. Provides descriptions of what teachers should look for and what they can do to be helpful.

Redmond, L. M. (1989). *Surviving: When someone you love was murdered.* Clearwater, FL: Psychological Consultation and Educational Services.

Addresses the special needs of persons grieving the death of someone who was murdered. Gives advice on establishing a community homicide survivors group and details a 12-session grief therapy program.

Audiovisual Materials

As we learn to fall: A look at death and grief and coping and living [videocassette]. Centre Productions, 12801 Schabarum Avenue, Irwindale, CA 91706.

This 30-minute video for grades 4 to 12 won the Gold Award from the Corporation for Public Broadcasting. It presents the stories of a teenager who struggles to accept the death of a friend and a cancer victim who dies at age 11. A guide with information about childhood grief and an extensive bibliography are included.

Blackberries in the dark [videocassette or 16 mm film]. (1988). Coronet/MTI Film & Video, 108 Wilmot Road, Deerfield, IL 60015.

Based on the novel by Mavis Jukes, this 26-minute video is suggested for grades 4 to 6. The story of how a 9-year-old struggles with the death of his grandfather encourages students to explore their own feelings about death and dying.

Dying is part of living [videocassette]. (1986). Sunburst Communications, Department AW, 39 Washington Avenue, Pleasantville, NY 10570.

This 40-minute, 3-part video, made from full-color slides, can be used with students, parents, and teachers to foster an understanding of how death affects teenagers. Illustrates many concepts of grief recovery theory.

The heart of the new age hospice [videocassette]. (1987). Carle Medical Communications, 110 West Main Street, Urbana, IL 61801.

This award winning, 28-minute video (produced by University of Texas TV) examines many aspects of hospice and offers a model for establishing a community-based program. Can be used with high school students and adults who may want to become hospice volunteers.

Suicide: A teenage dilemma [videocassette]. (1987). Health Sciences Consortium, 201 Silver Cedar Court, Chapel Hill, NC 27514.

This live action video will sensitize and educate teachers, school staff, and parents about teenage suicide. Useful in parent workshops or teacher in-service programs.

What do I tell my children? [videocassette]. (1986). Life Cycle Productions, P. O. Box 183ABCD, Newton, MA 02165.

This 30-minute video, narrated by Joanne Woodward, focuses on adults who experienced the death of a loved one when they were young children. Adults talk to children about how they reacted. Included are interviews with leading grief therapists, who stress the need for honesty when dealing with a grieving child. Useful as a training tool for teachers, counselors, and parents.

Support Groups

The Compassionate Friends

These groups for bereaved parents meet locally in many parts of the country. Members usually know about other support groups and programs, for example, those for grieving children or teenagers. For more information, contact a local mental health agency or the national headquarters, P. O. Box 3696, Oak Brook, IL 60522.

Parents of Murdered Children
& Other Survivors of Homicide Victims

Contact community mental health agencies for information about a local support group or the national POMC headquarters at 100 East 8th Street, Suite B-41, Cincinnati, OH 45202.

Sudden Infant Death Syndrome (SIDS) Support Group

Groups for parents and siblings of a child who died from SIDS meet locally in many cities. For information contact local hospitals, mental health agencies, or the National SIDS Foundation, 10500 Little Patuxent Parkway, Suite 420, Columbia, MD 21044.

Suicide Survivors Groups

Contact local community mental health agencies or request an updated directory of groups nationwide from the Suicide Prevention Center, Inc.,184 Salem Street, Dayton, OH 45406.

■ APPENDIX B ■

Forms and Other Materials

I. MEMORANDA FOR TEACHERS AND STAFF

Announcing a Teacher Death

TO: All faculty

FROM: _____ , Principal

DATE: _____

Please read the following announcement to students in your first period class:

As some of you may know, one of our teachers, Miss Brown, died yesterday. Although the exact reason for her death is not clear at this time, it was by natural causes. I know that this news may be very upsetting to some of you. If you need to talk with a counselor, you should let me know.

Suggestions for Helping Students

1. Be prepared for tears. Bring a box of tissues to class. Crying is a normal and healthy reaction, even though it may make you or some students uncomfortable.

2. Recognize that some students who are traumatized most by this news may be very quiet or seem to be in a daze. Be alert to this possibility and have these students escorted to the counseling office.

3. During first period, send grieving students to one of the following rooms: _(give room numbers)_ . A counseling professional and a teacher will be there to assist the students. After first period ends, send students who are upset to the counseling office.

4. During the day, you may, if you wish, let your students discuss this event or allow them to write about their feelings.

5. Just listening to students express their feelings and responding to the "hurt" is helpful. Supportive responses include:

"I can see that you are really hurting."

"It is very hard to accept the death of someone close."

"I know . . . it just seems unbelievable."

The following types of responses usually are not helpful:

"You will feel better tomorrow."

"I know just how you feel. When I lost my mother (brother, etc.), I thought I would never get over it, but I did."

Announcing an Accident Death

TO: All faculty

FROM: _____ , Principal

DATE: _____

Please read the following announcement to your first period class:

A 10th-grade student, Maria _____ *, died as the result of an automobile accident that occurred shortly after midnight Friday. Maria was killed instantly. Another student, Lori* _____ *, was seriously injured and is in Medical Center Hospital. We are all saddened by this news. If anyone needs to talk with a counselor, please let me know.*

The accident happened on _____ *Road. Apparently the car in which these girls were riding tried to avoid a car that approached them with its headlights off. Their car veered off the road and struck a large tree. The driver of the car and Lori were thrown from the car and seriously injured. Maria was trapped inside the car, where she died shortly after the crash.*

Suggestions for Helping Students

1. Be prepared for tears. Crying is a normal and healthy reaction, even though it may make you or some students uncomfortable.

2. Recognize that some students who are traumatized most by this news may be very quiet or seem to be in a daze. Be alert to this possibility and have someone bring these students to the counseling office.

3. Send grieving students to the counseling office. A counselor or a teacher will be there to assist them.

4. During the day, you may, if you wish, let your students discuss this event or allow them to write about their feelings.

5. Just listening to students express their feelings and responding to the "hurt" is helpful. Supportive responses include:

"I can see that you are really hurting."

"It is very hard to accept the death of someone you knew well."

"I know . . . it just seems unbelievable."
The following types of responses usually *are not* helpful:
"You will feel better tomorrow." "Don't think about it now."
"A friend of mine died when I was your age and I got over it."

Announcing a Suspected, but Unconfirmed, Suicide Death

TO: All faculty

FROM: _____ , Principal

DATE: _____

Please read the following announcement to students in your first period class:

We are saddened to learn of the death this weekend of one of our students, Juan _____ . *Juan died Saturday afternoon of a gunshot wound. The complete details of his death are not available at this time. I know that this news may be upsetting to some of you. If you need to talk with a counselor, please let me know. I will give you a pass to the counseling office.*

Suggestions for Helping Students

(Note: Refer to previous memorandum for information that was included in this section.)

If you have first or second period conference, please go to the counseling office to see if your assistance is needed. A counselor will follow Juan's class schedule to meet with his classmates throughout the day. If I feel that any further action is needed in response to this death, I will call a faculty meeting or will send you a memorandum.

(Note: Although it was common knowledge among students at this school that Juan shot himself at his home, the coroner had not ruled the death a suicide. If it had been ruled suicide, the announcement would have read: *"died . . . of a self-inflicted gunshot wound."*)

Announcing a Suicide Death

The suicide of a student, particularly one who was well known or popular, can produce campuswide trauma if the death occurs when school is in session. In announcing the death, it may be helpful to include information about the grieving process and sources of assistance. The following example was adapted from an announcement prepared in 1988 by Robert Enos, an Austin, Texas, high school principal. (It was shared with the author by the district's crisis coordinator, Dr. Betty Phillips).

The _____ school community is saddened by the reported suicide of one of our students. The death of any member of a community is a loss that in one way or another diminishes each of us, but the tragic circumstances of _____'s death are more difficult to accept. Feelings of anger, hurt, depression, and guilt are natural following a suicide. We may wonder what we could have done to prevent this act of desperation. Although feeling guilt is natural, none of us can assume responsibility because the ultimate decision was not ours to make. There is, however, something each of us can do. You, as students, can assist your friends and classmates. Your teachers, counselors, and administrators are here to help all students, whatever the problem. If you, or one of your friends, need to talk, let a teacher or counselor know. Both students and faculty can be alert for others who need help. Often, a friendly smile, an offer to have lunch together, a word of encouragement, or just listening can make a difference. Whether we realize it or not, we do need each other.

Following the announcement, teachers may lead class discussions or send students to previously determined areas for counseling.

Announcing a Death That Occurred in the Summer

The following memorandum was given to teachers before the first day of school concerning a student who killed himself in August. At a preschool in-service meeting, the principal advised teachers to make this announcement *only* if students seemed upset or asked for information. In this instance, the principal *chose to ignore the event* (see the section on determining degree of trauma in chapter 2). If the death had occurred during the school year, it would not have been ignored. Because only a few students were upset the first day of school, the chosen response proved appropriate. These students were counseled individually and referred to the school's grief support group.

***

TO: All faculty

FROM: _____ , Principal

DATE: _____

Read the following announcement only if there seems to be a need (i.e., students request information about the death or seem upset.)

Sam _____ , *who would have been a senior this fall, died on August 15 of a self-inflicted gunshot wound. A memorial service was held August 17 at the* _____ *Funeral Home. If you find this news upsetting, you may want to talk with your counselor.*

The counselors will offer a loss and grief support group beginning next week for interested students. A workshop for concerned parents may also be held. Information about these activities is available in the counseling office.

***

TEACHERS: As most of you know, loss and grief groups are offered each year for students grieving the death of a relative or friend. Please notify the counseling office of students who may profit from the group. The parent workshop on student suicide may be of interest to you as teachers or parents. Descriptions of the student group and parent workshop are available in the teachers' lounge.

II. LETTER TO PARENTS

Following some deaths, the principal communicates with parents by mail and/or public forums. A sample letter to be used following a student suicide is given below. A similar letter may be needed after a homicide death or tragic accident.

***

Dear Parents:

The _____ school community has been saddened by the suicide death of one of our students, _____ .
I want to let you know what steps we are taking to assist our grieving students. *(Describe what actions are being taken.)*

You can expect that your child will be affected in some way by this tragedy even if he or she did not know this student well. I encourage you to talk to your child about what happened. Discussing thoughts and feelings about death is important to the resolution of grief. You will not "put ideas into your child's head" by talking about suicide. We all need to reinforce, however, that such actions are foolish and that there is help for any problem. Encourage your child to talk to you or some other adult when life stresses become overwhelming. If you are concerned about your child, please contact (staff person) at (phone number) .

I have enclosed an information sheet that may help you understand and respond to your child's feelings. *(Enclose information about helpful responses, how students this age react to death, and warning signs of depression or at-risk behaviors.)*

A meeting for concerned parents will be held _____ _____ . *(If a meeting is planned, give the details.)*

If you have any questions concerning this incident or the actions we are taking, please call my office. You are an important part of our school community and your child's life.

Sincerely,

_____ , Principal

Enclosures

***

III. COUNSELING GROUP NOTICES

The following information is printed on school letterhead.

❦

Parent Permission Form

TO: The parents of _____

FROM: _____ , Principal (or counselor)

    There are loss events in the lives of young people (or children) that cause them to grieve. The counseling staff at _____ _____ school offers a loss and grief support group to help our students process their feelings and learn to cope with future losses. Your son/daughter wants to participate in this group.

    The group meets once a week for 8 weeks. Students in the group will not miss any class *(or subject if elementary school group)* more than twice during that time. The group has a learning component and a sharing component. Topics covered usually include the following:

    1. Types of losses;
    2. Stages of grief recovery;
    3. Identifying, normalizing, and sharing feelings,
    4. Healthy versus unhealthy grief responses;
    5. Recognizing and coping with depression; and
    6. Myths about grief.

    Please sign and return the form below if you give permission for your son/daughter to participate in this group. If you have any questions, please call _____ at _____

My son/daughter _____ may participate in the loss and grief support group.

_____   _____
(Parent Signature)   (Date)

❦

Notice to Prospective Group Members

TO: ___(prospective group member)___

FROM: _____ , Counselor

    I will begin a **Loss and Grief Support Group** soon. This group is for students who have had someone close to them die—a friend, a parent, grandparent, or other close relative. Some of these deaths may have occurred recently and others may have happened years ago. Your name was given to me by your counselor or a teacher who thought that you might want to be in this group.

    These groups are held each semester at _____ _____ school. The students who participate always report that the group was helpful and they recommend it for others. Students learn about the grief process and how to help themselves and others cope with loss. We meet during the school day, one period a week for 8 weeks.

    I would like to talk to you about joining the group. I look forward to meeting with you soon.

Teacher Notification Form

TO: ___(each teacher of group members)___

FROM: _____ , Counselor

_____(name of student)_____ , who is in your _____
period class, will be in my spring **Loss and Grief Support Group.**
He/she will miss your class **only twice** on _____
(dates) _____ . Please excuse this student to attend the
group unless you have a major test planned. Please see me if
you have any questions.

This form is sent to group members on the day the group meets, even though they were given a schedule of meeting times at the first group session and their teachers have been notified.

⟡

Reminder to Group Members

TO: _____(group member)_____

FROM: _____ , Counselor

The loss support group meets today _____(date)_____ during _____ period (*or give time*). Please go to your class to remind your teacher that you will be absent. Then, come quickly to room _____. This form will serve as your hall pass.

⟡

IV. GRIEF RESOLUTION INVENTORY
By Martha Oates, Ed.D., Counselor

Instructions: Think about the death you experienced. Place a check in the blank under your answer to each question.

Most of the time	**Some of the time**	**Not at all or rarely**	
____	____	____	1. Can you talk about this loss without becoming upset?
____	____	____	2. Can you think about how your life was before this loss without feeling a great deal of emotional pain?
____	____	____	3. Do you feel angry, either at a specific person or just angry in general, when you think of this loss?
____	____	____	4. Are you generally happy and look forward to the future and the good things it will bring you?
____	____	____	5. Can you go places that remind you of this loss without being overly upset or feeling depressed?
____	____	____	6. Do you still think or say "If only . . ." about this death?
____	____	____	7. Do you remember this person's good points **and** his/her bad ones?
____	____	____	8. Do you feel guilty about your prior relationship with this person or about any of the events that caused the death?

Score your inventory as follows:

a. Assign three (3) points for each check under
"most of the time" for questions 1, 2, 4, 5, and 7.   _____

b. Assign three (3) points for each check under
"not at all or rarely" for questions 3, 6, and 8.   _____

c. Add one (1) point for each check under "some
of the time."

                                                          _____

                                              Total: _____

A score of 18–24 usually means that a person is experiencing a healthy resolution of grief. Anyone who scores below 18 may profit from participation in a grief support group. A score below 12 may indicate a need for grief counseling.

V. SUPPORT GROUP EVALUATION FORM

Directions to group members: Please complete the following statements to assist us in evaluating this group experience. Use the back of this sheet if you need more space for your answers.

1. One thing I learned from this group is . . .

2. When I began this group I thought/felt . . .

3. Now I think/feel . . .

4. The best thing about this group was . . .

5. This type of group could be improved by . . .

6. Would you recommend this group to other students? Why or why not?

THANKS FOR YOUR HELP AND FOR BEING A PART OF THIS GROUP.

Please remember that this is a library book,
and that it belongs only temporarily to each
person who uses it. Be considerate. Do
not write in this, or any, library book.